Calming Anxiety

A Comprehensive Guide to Understanding and Managing Anxiety

Library of Congress Cataloging in Publication Data
ISBN 979-8-9936303-0-4

INSIGHT GROVE
PUBLISHING

www.InsightGrovePublishing.com

Contents

Introduction

Anxiety is such a thing that it is almost impossible to find a human who has not been affected at least once during their lifetime. In such cases, it could be nervousness before a speech delivery, worrying about the health of our relatives, or feeling anxiety that seems to come out of nowhere, leaving one unable to help oneself. It is paradoxical that anxiety, being one of our most common, shared experiences, is still something that most people are silent about, if not wholly unaware of the occurring situation, and have no clue how to get better.

The author of this book aims for it to be a constant companion for the reader, evident in its exploration of the wilderness of anxiety. It guides the reader from understanding its origin to realizing initial tools for cohabitation, allowing you to continue with enriched self-care in your daily routine. Through this journey, you will learn that anxiety is a system that is not in your favor. In fact, it is a network that, with proper comprehension and management, will enable you to use it as a helpful guide to what you need and the limits you want.

You will be introduced to a range of topics related to anxiety. Over time, your ability to understand and manage your anxiety will undoubtedly improve.

As a matter of fact, no matter if you are the type of person whose anxiety occurs sporadically and at rare moments, or you have the problem of anxiety that is so persistent that it even interferes with your life, this book is always there to offer you its help in the form of strategies that are based on evidence that you will be able to control and be at peace with yourself again. The idea is not to eradicate anxiety from the face of the earth; that would be neither feasible nor preferable. Instead, it is to work on creating a healthier connection with it.

Remember, your journey with anxiety is uniquely yours. This book is a map, offering guidance and support, but the path you choose and the treatments you find most effective are what truly matter.

The Many Faces of Anxiety

Beyond the Stereotype

When people think about anxiety, they picture someone suffering from a panic attack - breathing rapidly, sweating a lot, and feeling as if having a heart attack. Although a panic attack is one of the ways anxiety can occur, it is only a small number of cases related to the anxiety continuum. The different faces of anxiety are many, and to comprehend its other characteristics is to be able to manage them to a great extent.

Jackson is sitting in his office, appearing calm and bright to the other workers. However, the reality is that his brain is busy running through the worst-case scenarios for the customer meeting tomorrow. Without being adequately prepared, he has already rehearsed seventeen different ways the presentation could have gone wrong.

Anita doesn't attend parties; it's not that she dislikes people, but rather the thought of conversation terrifies her. Before every social event, she dedicates hours to conversation analysis, worrying about silence and devising ways to avoid embarrassing herself. Her anxiety is in the form of escape and seclusion from the party rather than thinking about having a nice time.

Jeff is constantly watching his phone for any new information he cannot wait to receive. At the same time, every notification pushes adrenaline through his body as he waits for the worst to happen. He is consumed by worries about the state of the world, fearing disasters, political instability, and economic collapse. His anxiety is manifesting in an information addiction and a failure to unplug from global issues.

Anxiety shows itself differently in these examples. Knowing these differences is important because it allows you to recognize anxiety not only in yourself but also in people around you, to eliminate the feeling of embarrassment since the different ways anxiety shows itself have become a common thing, and depending on the anxiety, to get the proper ways of managing one's time and self.

Generalized Anxiety: The Persistent Worrier

Generalized Anxiety Disorder, or GAD, is mainly about being worried, being anxious to an extreme degree, and focusing on life aspects that most people consider trivial.

Whereas phobias limit anxieties to one particular thing, such as an object or a situation, GAD stretches the anxiety net far and wide. GAD patients may worry about their jobs, families, health, money, global matters, and so on – making a long list of topics they usually worry about at the same time.

Commonly, the concern in GAD is often exaggerated regarding how much people think about it compared to how real the feared events actually become.

A person experiencing GAD might end up spending a lot of time worrying about the most minor incidents until they make them much bigger than it is. Often, generalized anxiety will cause sleep disturbances, such as lying awake and worrying about their child getting harmed at school, although there is no sign of danger.

What is even more complicated about GAD is that it is not only difficult to spot but also challenging to overcome, as it is pervasive. Contrarily, a person with a specific phobia can quite easily escape the place where their trigger is, while with generalized anxiety, it is almost impossible to detach oneself from a particular topic and not be prone to anxiety surrounding it majestically. Once one worry is gone, a new one is already there. One anxious thought may bring you to another, which in turn brings you yet another, thus an interminable 'what if' scenario cycle.

People with generalized anxiety often say that they feel as if they are constantly in a state of expecting the worst to happen. They may sometimes struggle to relax. They find that even when engaging in pleasant activities, their brains are always on the lookout for potential problems. Being constantly on guard can be quite a drain and can also affect their sleep, concentration, and overall well-being, including their ability to live with joy.

The physical symptoms of generalized anxiety most of the time consist of muscle tension, especially in the areas of the neck, shoulders, and jaw. Headaches, fatigue, an upset stomach, and trouble sleeping are common symptoms.

Besides that, most people report feeling restless. They believe their energy is high or that they are on the verge of nervousness, making it difficult for them to sit still or completely relax.

The thinking patterns associated with GAD primarily involve tendencies to overestimate the likelihood of adverse events and underestimate one's ability to cope with them. Those with GAD are frequently engaged in deeply complex mental problem-solving where they try to foresee and plan for every single possible thing that can go wrong. The fact that it may only be slightly helpful does not stop them from continuing in this way, without actually solving the problems, which eventually leads to mental exhaustion.

Panic Disorder: Terror Without Warning

One of the most energetic anxiety forms is panic attacks. Panic attacks do not go by unnoticed, as the body's alarm system is on full throttle, making a person experience symptoms so extreme that a lot of them, probably the majority, think that they are having a heart attack, stroke, or any other medical emergency. The list of physical symptoms that can accompany a panic attack includes feelings of sweating, trembling, shortness of breath, rapid heartbeat, chest pain, nausea, dizziness, hot or cold flashes, and numbness or tingling sensations.

The feature of a panic attack is the overwhelming power and the sensation of losing control. The person is often found to say they are going mad, they are dying, or they are being destroyed forever. The symptoms may be at their strongest in a few minutes, but they can seem like hours to a person experiencing them.

Panic disorder starts growing when a person is frightened of experiencing panic attacks. The loop where more panic attacks are triggered by the fear of experiencing panic, leading to a further panic reaction. People who have panic disorder usually tend to develop agoraphobia, which is the fear of places and situations from which it is difficult or embarrassing to escape when a panic attack happens. This might result in avoiding crowded areas, driving, traveling, or even leaving your home.

One of the worst things about panic attacks is the fact that you never know when they will strike. Though in some cases people may be able to point out the causes of their attacks, most times, panic attacks seem to be totally unexpected, thus, a feeling of being on edge all the time. This constant focusing on how the body feels can lead to more panic attacks because the typical signs of the body (for example, a fast heartbeat after jogging) are taken as signs of the coming panic attack.

A pitiful feature of panic disorder is that the panic attacks, apart from being scary, are not fatal. The symptoms themselves are perceived as life-threatening, but they don't cause any harm to the body. But to be honest, this understanding only makes the experience less frightening in the moment.

Social Anxiety: The Fear of Judgment

Social anxiety is the intense fear of social situations in which one might be observed or evaluated by others. It is not just shyness or an occasional feeling of discomfort. For a person suffering from this condition, even the simplest social interactions may seem like tests where they expect to fail and be rejected, embarrassed, or isolated from the rest of society.

Probably the scariest layer in the social anxiety issue is the fear that others would evaluate them negatively. If we look at this fear from a practical point of view, it is about not being seen as a hypocrite in one's words, not appearing nervous or awkward, not being perceived as boring or worthless, and not being rejected or excluded. Due to the vicious circle that characterizes the problem, these people often fail in their social interactions, which consequently leads to increased fear.

Some examples of physical symptoms include blushing, sweating, trembling, voice alterations, or an empty feeling in the mind at critical times.

Social anxiety may be a diverse, general problem that affects almost all social situations, or it can be an isolated, specific problem, only occurring in some instances, such as public speaking, eating in front of others, or using restrooms in public places. The severity may range from a minor impact on a person's life, which remains within the individual's control, to significant problems that profoundly affect their social and professional life.

People who have social anxiety usually tend to excessively plan what they are going to do before coming to a social event, do mental rehearsal of the conversations, analyze and critique themselves after the event, and also avoid social situations. Furthermore, they may also use subtle avoidance methods, such as avoiding eye contact or looking at exits that will help you get away quickly.

It is the paradox of social anxiety that it very often does not allow the sufferers to access the positive social experiences through which the anxiety naturally diminishes. Avoiding anxiety-causing situations is what keeps the anxiety going, as it deprives the person of the experiences that could disprove it.

Specific Phobias: Intense Fear of Particular Things

Phobias embody intense and irrational fears, which individuals experience towards specific objects, situations, or activities. The most common phobias are spiders, snakes, blood, needles, dogs, closed spaces, heights, and flying and driving. Typically, the fear is no less than many times disproportionate to the potential danger that comes from the phobic stimulus.

Phobia is differentiated from normal fear or dislike primarily by its avoidance and intensity features. The reaction from the side of fear in terms of a phobia can also be so great that it may lead the person to go to extraordinary lengths to avoid the situation. Thus, a person with a spider phobia may not enter a basement where it is likely to be dark and spiders may be lurking, or a person with a flying phobia may opt for a very long land trip instead of a short two-hour flight.

One direct traumatic experience, in which the person was scared of the particular thing, is enough to have them fear it for the whole of their lives, and they are also capable of developing the phobia through observational learning, which is the seeing of another's fear reactions, and informational learning (hearing about).

There are cases when they seem to develop into phobias without any apparent reason. This may be because we are biologically predisposed to fear things that were dangerous for our ancestors more quickly than those that were not.

As a result of those phobias, the affected persons avoid some places or participating in activities that they think will be dangerous or stressful to them. For instance, a person with a fear of elevators will likely never visit high-rise offices, so they will only accept jobs in single-floor buildings. After work, going upstairs home on foot is the only way to go. The person with a phobia of driving may rely on friends with cars for his travel or only go to places where he can walk safely.

Health Anxiety: The Fear of Illness

Health anxiety is sometimes called hypochondriasis or illness anxiety disorder and is a condition in which there are severe concerns about acquiring or having serious medical conditions. Those with health anxiety tend to view standard body signals in the worst light as signs of a severe disease, and thus, they do a lot of self-checking. This may include self-examination, compulsive internet searching, or a constant need for medical reassurance, which they seek by consulting different doctors.

Regular health anxiety follows the pattern of the person's life, noticing a somatic feeling in the body. Common examples include a headache, chest tightness, or stomach upset. The physical feeling is then taken to a worst-case scenario: 'This headache is probably a brain tumor,' or 'This chest tightness means that I am having a heart attack.'

Such reasoning leads to the symptom of anxiety. In return, the newly arisen physical symptoms (rapid heartbeat, sweating, muscle tension) are then interpreted as additional proof of a severe disease.

Patients with health anxiety may jump to the point where they know everything about the different conditions that medicine has. They may spend a considerable amount of time reading through medical topics online or consulting medical books. Ironically, this research for potential solutions quite frequently results in anxiety growth rather than a drop because they come across more disorders to be afraid of or more symptoms to watch.

On an interesting side note, nursing and medical students often will develop some form of hypochondriacal stress during their first year of study. It usually occurs when the student perceives themselves as experiencing the symptoms of a disease they are studying. This is often due to a perceptual process and not a psychopathology.

At most, medical support can only lessen the load of worry for a limited time. Actually, when a doctor tells the person with health anxiety that everything is fine, the relief doesn't last long, and soon after, a new symptom or a new conception pops up, and the cycle repeats.

Obsessive-Compulsive Disorder: Anxiety's Elaborate Rituals

OCD is currently considered to be a separate group apart from anxiety disorders; still, it has similarities with anxiety and is commonly found together with anxiety disorders. The main features of OCD are persistent, unwanted thoughts (obsessions) and repetitive, ritualized behaviors or mental acts (compulsions) that are done to lower the anxiety or stop the feared consequences.

Obsessions commonly include the idea of contamination, worrying that one might get sick or that one will harm oneself or others, the need for symmetry or exactness, and forbidden or taboo thoughts concerning sex, religion, or violence. Compulsions may also involve excessive washing or cleaning, along with additional behaviors performed to alleviate the distress of the obsession, such as checking, counting, and repeating prayers or phrases.

The connection between obsessions and compulsions is not straightforward. Obsessive anxiety induces the need for the compulsive act to reduce the anxiety temporarily (What if I did not lock the door and someone breaks in?) or (I will recheck the lock). However, this relief is only temporary; the obsessive thought returns, usually more powerful than it was before.

OCD can limit a person's time and function severely to the point that it becomes difficult to do daily activities. Some individuals may find themselves compelled to spend hours performing repetitive behaviors each day, while intrusive thoughts can be so harrowing that focusing becomes a significant challenge.

The content of obsessions frequently clashes with the values of the people they belong to, making the affected individuals more upset and ashamed than before.

Post-Traumatic Stress: When Danger Lingers

Post-Traumatic Stress Disorder (PTSD) originates in a person after they have been exposed to or have seen very traumatic events. Nevertheless, not every traumatized person will end up having PTSD. Symptoms of the illness, however, can be so severe that they significantly impair the daily functioning of individuals affected by it.

The symptoms of PTSD are intrusive with re-experiencing of the trauma (through flashbacks, nightmares, or unbidden memories), avoidance of trauma-related stimuli, changes in arousal and reactivity, and negative alterations in thoughts and mood. Reminders of the traumatic event mostly trigger anxiety in PTSD, although it can also be generalized.

Hypervigilance typically accompanies PTSD, and an individual remains in a state of very close watch, scanning for potential threats even in a secure location. It is essentially the experience of being caught in a never-ending, exhausting, and demanding state of one's nervous system, which can lead to problems with sleep, concentration, and relationships. The environment no longer appears dangerous, and the person's system for identifying danger is always functioning.

Besides these, PTSD symptoms may include survivor's guilt, emotional numbing, trouble feeling positive emotions, memory issues, and concentration issues. Personal relationships often struggle since the person finds it difficult to trust others or become emotionally involved.

Separation Anxiety: The Fear of Losing Connection
Although it is a characteristic that is most prominent in children, separation anxiety is a disorder that can be found in individuals of any age. This disorder is accompanied by an irrational fear of being away from the people the person is attached to or the places the person is familiar with. An adult may manifest this as being extremely worried when a spouse is traveling for work, not being able to spend time alone, or feeling anxious about the children being far from home.

Typically, separation anxiety is characterized by the person having thoughts that are very negative and imagining the worst-case scenarios while they are separated. The person might think of the most terrible things that could happen to the people they love, such as accidents, illnesses, or other disasters. When they are expecting to be separated or separation is in process, they may suffer from physical symptoms like nausea, headaches, or sleep troubles, which are pretty standard.

The individuals with separation anxiety disorder are usually scared only in situations when they are about to be separated or are already separated. A person is generally calm and feels safe when they are with the people they are attached to. This can serve as an indication of separation anxiety from generalized anxiety disorder, where the anxiety is more widespread and is not so specific.

Performance Anxious: The Spotlight Effect

One gets performance anxiety only when one's abilities are to be judged or seen. Situations like these occur during tests, sports competitions, musical concerts, job interviews, and public talks. The fear of evaluation, failure, or embarrassment is the source of this anxiety.

Performance anxiety frequently leads to tragic irony, which is that the anxiety can become a performance-impairing factor. A person with test anxiety may experience a complete mental blank during the exam, a victim of stage fright may do things he is not accustomed to, and interview anxiety can make one look less competent than he really is.

Among them, the performance anxiety physical symptoms can be most vexing because they are quite often visible to the people around. Shaking hands, a trembling voice, blushing, or sweating can be both embarrassing and anxiety-inducing.

Furthermore, this creates a feedback loop where individuals aware of the symptoms become more anxious, which in turn intensifies the symptoms.

Existential Anxiety: Questions Without Answers

The most usual causes of existential anxiety are the questions. What is the purpose of life? What happens after death? Am I doing the right thing? Does anything matter at all? The game of life undergoes a significant shift when an anxious, existential person reaches the point of losing, resting, or reflecting.

Other types of anxiety differ in that they concentrate on the concrete threats of the world, but existential anxiety deals with the uncertainty of the world and the limitedness of human beings. Trying to find answers and, at the same time, really not being sure, and then seeking help is the trademark of existential anxiety, making it hard to control. For example, existential anxiety might show through depression, anomie, or an aversive feeling towards an ocean of life's possibilities and duties.

Mixed Presentations: When Anxiety Wears Multiple Masks

Multiple presentations are when you experience more than one anxiety type, and their mix is different but often equal. The change of presentations over time is possible. Consider that a person could suffer from generalized anxiety that, however, at times, becomes so strong that panic attacks are felt. Or he might have social anxiety complicated with health anxiety, which causes him to be very anxious about the visible symptoms of nervousness.

Moreover, it is perfectly normal for the anxiety condition to move from one area of concern to another. For example, an individual may become free from a specific phobia and then quickly develop health anxiety, or their generalized anxiety may get worse but be more concentrated on social issues in times of crisis.

Knowing that anxiety can show in different forms as well as new combinations of symptoms contributes to understanding the nature of anxiety complexity. Additionally, it accentuates the significance of the personalized treatment protocols, which implies that the therapy for panic disorder might be less effective for social anxiety.

The Hidden Forms

Some signs of anxiety are less visible, and the people may not be fully aware of them, even as they experience anxiety. Putting things off, as an example, is primarily related to anxiety over one's performance, failure, or being judged. Perfectionism is often a way of controlling one's anxiety about making errors or letting others down. Irritability and anger are some of the signs of anxiety that can be present, especially when the person is feeling overwhelmed or in a losing position, and thus, becomes upset and frustrated.

Workaholism could be a disguise for anxieties over financial security or professional skills. People-pleasing habits may be a result of social anxiety and a fear of rejection. Even some kinds of depression might include significant anxiety elements, especially when the depression is about worrying about the future or overthinking past events.

It is essential to identify these disguised anxiety disorders because they can be a source of prolific dissatisfaction with life, and they can function just as much as the more evident ones. Anxiety can also coexist with several common comorbidities. As a result, they can only be managed successfully if the management moves include a general relaxation of anxiety as a trigger of other disorders.

Cultural and Individual Variations

There are significant and even individual differences between the way anxiety is experienced in different cultures. Some cultures may be more open to expressing feelings, while others may be more reserved. Some view anxiety as a medical issue that requires the assistance of a doctor to address, while others regard it as a natural part of life or a spiritual struggle.

The anxiety manifestations are also affected by the individual aspects such as personality, genetics, life experiences, and social support. Some anxious individuals may choose to avoid situations that make them nervous or seek reassurance from others. While others may worry and experience physical symptoms during anxiety.

Moreover, factors such as gender, age, and socioeconomic status may also affect the expression of anxiety. Research shows that women are more likely to be diagnosed with anxiety disorders than men, but this could be a reflection of differences in the way women and men approach help-seeking, symptom expression, or diagnostic bias rather than actual prevalence differences.

The Importance of Professional Assessment

This book can serve as a handbook in the world of anxiety. While the book shows the various faces of anxiety, a professional assessment will always be more definitive in establishing a precise diagnosis and a clear treatment plan. Mental health providers in the field of mental affliction are equipped to differentiate the variations of anxiousness, spot overlapping parts of different maladies that co-occur, and prescribers may need to suggest the proper medication.

Furthermore, self-diagnosing based on the information you find in books or on the internet can lead to mistakes since numerous symptoms in different conditions overlap, and sometimes what looks like anxiety may in fact be an entirely different condition. Besides that, medical checkups to ascertain that there are no bodily diseases that can mimic or aggravate anxiety symptoms may be crucial.

Finding Your Pattern

If you decided to go through these different representations of anxiety and you found some features of your own experience, you are on the right track. This kind of acknowledgment can be immensely comforting. It lets the idea sink in that your struggles, no matter how hard, are neither unique nor unheard. What is more, it can become your first move towards dealing with anxiety in a more personalized manner.

Please identify which descriptions of the disorder best align with your experience and will help you understand it better. Could you mainly identify yourself with one group, or are you discovering traits in several categories? Has your anxiety depiction changed over time? Recognizing your personal pattern is the foundation for developing your own coping strategies.

When you reflect that no matter how anxiety got inside, it doesn't tell you what type of person you are, don't forget that you are way more than that. It is not who you are, but what you suffer from. Through comprehension, use of correct measures, and patience with yourself, you can manage anxiety's intrusion in your life and, at the same time, be respectful of its aid-providing features.

The upcoming chapter will teach you ways of recognizing your own anxiety triggers and situations by tracing back through the basics of understanding the numerous faces of anxiety. As a result of this investigation, you will be able to create a customized anxiety relief plan that caters specifically to your needs and the requirements of your environment.

The Science of Anxiety – Brain & Body

Understanding The Architecture of Fear

Anxiety is not a mere mental or emotional state, but also a complex biological phenomenon that consists of the complicated networks of brain regions, chemical messengers, and bodily systems working together. To understand anxiety properly, we must first recognize the remarkable evolutionary mechanisms that have sustained our species for thousands of years, while also acknowledging how this ancient system can sometimes harm us in our contemporary world.

The anxiety reaction in humans is one of the most complex survival mechanisms that nature has evolved. For example, if our ancestors came across a predator while they were on the savanna, their survival would have relied upon an instant change of their entire physiology, as a result of which their brains would have assessed the danger, supplied the body with necessary chemicals, and prepared all the muscles, organs, and systems for immediate reaction. Today, this very same mechanism is at work inside us, but the "predators" are more like job interviews, social situations, or financial pressures.

The Brain's Anxiety Network

Located deep within the anxiety brain network is a cluster of different brain structures that have evolved over a vast timespan. Identifying these regions and their connections is a significant step in understanding why anxiety is the way it is and why it is so hard to defeat by mere willpower.

The Amygdala: The Brain's Alarm System

The amygdala is a small, almond-shaped structure located deep within the brain's limbic system, which serves as our primary threat detection center. These early structures are competent in their work. They can pinpoint threats and react by arming the body in as little as 12 milliseconds, which is significantly before our conscious mind even understands what is happening.

The amygdala errs on the side of safety, which means it quite often yields one or more false alarms. Such a bias in favor of overreaction is logical if we consider the forefathers, who might have been more successful in survival by jumping at shadows rather than neglecting possible threats. Though in this new world, this razor-sharp response may become the source of anxiety disorders in cases when the amygdala is over-sensitive and starts to perceive everyday situations as life threats.

The amygdala is not only a threat detector but also a storehouse of emotional memories associated with frightening situations. It explains why we can feel the anxiety getting bigger whenever a particular smell, sound, or situation is present. Yet, that memory of the reason behind the feeling of anxiety evades us. The amygdala has formed a network of memories that bypasses our logic and directly triggers the fear we experience.

The Hippocampus: Memory and Context

The hippocampus is a seahorse-shaped structure essential for forming and recalling memories. It enables humans to construct memories, allowing them to differentiate between real dangers and false alarms based on previous experiences and the current state of the environment.

If all goes well with the hippocampus, it becomes a tool for the amygdala in assessing the truth of the case. Based on what we know about our location and typical sounds in that area, we can acknowledge that the sound in the bushes is probably just the wind, not a predator. In the meantime, continuous stress and anxiety may lead to the shrinkage of the hippocampus, and this will result in the loss of the utmost function of the hippocampus in giving contextual information and triggering fewer false alarms.

The connection between the hippocampus and anxiety is two-way. The hippocampus can be injured by anxiety, but a damaged hippocampus can also make anxiety worse by being unable to give proper background information for situations that might be threatening. This way, there is a loop where anxiety causes more anxiety.

The Prefrontal Cortex: The Rational Mind

The prefrontal cortex, located just behind our forehead, is the latest addition by evolution to the network of brain regions responsible for anxiety. The primary function of this part is to serve as the center for rationale, planning, and emotional regulation in the brain. The brain's CEO is one of the most frequently made comparisons, as it helps the central control system integrate and organize the functions of other brain areas.

When anxiety is the main reason, the prefrontal cortex is like an emergency brake system sent to the amygdala. When we calm ourselves down through taking a deep breath, grounding ourselves in reality, and rationally assessing the situation, we are utilizing our prefrontal cortex to silence the alarm signals sent by our amygdala. This area prompts us to consider whether the threat is real or imaginary.

Despite all of this, the prefrontal cortex is also the part that suffers from stress or anxiety, with a decrease in blood flow, and resources are redirected from this region to less developed or more primitive survival brain areas. This explains why it becomes so difficult for us to think clearly or make rational decisions when anxiety has us in its grasp.

The Anterior Cingulate Cortex: Emotional Processing

The anterior cingulate cortex (ACC) serves as a connector between our emotional and cognitive brain systems. This region serves as the central processor for the emotional significance of events, facilitating the integration of emotions with the rational thinking part of the brain.

The ACC in people with anxiety disorders may exhibit different activity patterns. It can be overly active in identifying potential threats, or it might not adequately control the flow of information between emotional and reasoning brain systems. The trouble with this part of the brain can become a source of constant worry and emotional pain, which are the main features of anxiety disorders.

Neural Pathways: The Information Superhighways

These brain regions are not separable units. The interconnected network of neural pathways allows them to communicate with each other very quickly. The speed and efficiency of these connections can significantly affect the time and the strength of anxiety that we can feel.

One of the most significant pathways is the direct connection between sensation and the amygdala. The so-called "low road" enables the amygdala to get threat-related signaling only just before other brain regions. This feature explains why we can be scared by a dark figure even though it turns out to be harmless.

In contrast to the low road, the "high road" involves processing in the higher cortex before reaching the amygdala. The assessment via this path is longer but more detailed. The interaction of these two methods of trial is very decisive in their impact on our anxiety symptoms.

The Chemical Messengers of Anxiety

The brain structures identify the hardware for anxiety responses; neurotransmitters and hormones act as the software—the command chains of the brain that implement these responses. Knowing these chemicals and the mechanism by which they operate is a step towards clearing the facts that anxiety is experienced the way it is, and also that some medications can be successfully utilized in the treatment of anxiety disorders.

GABA: The Brain's Natural Tranquilizer

Gamma-aminobutyric acid (GABA) is the brain's primary inhibitory neurotransmitter. In simple terms, its function is to calm the nerve cells and prevent the body from being excessively stimulated. GABA can be compared to the car's brake system in the brain. It enables one to regain control of the mind during panic attacks and diminishes the overexcitability of brain cells.

GABA is the neurotransmitter that balances the activity of excitatory neurotransmitters in the brain, maintaining stable homeostasis. People who suffer from anxiety disorders commonly face issues with GABA function. They are prone to a lack of GABA production, suffer from GABA receptor problems, and have genetic variations that influence GABA function.

This is also the main reason why a lot of anxiety drugs, such as benzodiazepines, work through the mechanism of GABA, similarly to the action of benzodiazepines like Xanax and Valium that act via GABA. These medications actually create a synergy between the brain's natural calming system. But still, the brain can build up a tolerance to these effects, which is why benzodiazepines are usually prescribed for only short-term use.

Serotonin: The Mood Stabilizer

Helped to be recognized as one of the leading players in the depression story, serotonin also plays a vital role in anxiety regulation. This neurotransmitter is the body's primary regulator of mood, sleep, nutrition, and anxiety. Most (around 90%) of the serotonin is actually released by the gut, indicating a clear relationship between digestive health and mental health.

With respect to anxiety, serotonin is a conductor that controls the nervous signals going to different parts of the brain involved in fear and worry. The sensation of tranquility and welfare accompanies Serotonin at the right level, while low serotonin can be a source of both anxiety and depression. This is the main reason why selective serotonin reuptake inhibitors (SSRIs) like Citalopram (Celexa), Escitalopram (Lexapro), Fluoxetine (Prozac), Fluvoxamine (Luvox), Paroxetine (Paxil), Sertraline (Zoloft), and others elevate the content of serotonin available in the brain, are frequently put on the list first in the treatment of anxiety disorders.

Serotonin is a multifaceted system consisting of different receptor groups both in the brain and outside it. Not only that, but even different serotonin receptors may have different roles regarding anxiety; some may decrease anxiety, while others increase anxiety.

This property of the serotonin system clarifies why, in some cases, patients who take serotonin-based drugs have initial anxiety followed by relief.

Norepinephrine: The Alertness Chemical

The substance norepinephrine, also known as noradrenaline, serves as both a neurotransmitter in the brain and a hormone in the rest of the body. Its most important function is to make a person alert and thus prepare them to take some action. Nonetheless, the positive side of it is the negative side if uncontrolled, when an overactivity of the norepinephrine system is directly linked to panic attacks and anxiety disorders.

As the brain perceives the threat, norepinephrine levels surge, resulting in an increased heart rate, heightened awareness, and an energizing effect on the rest of the body. This chemical is linked to most of the physical symptoms of anxiety, such as rapid heartbeat, profuse perspiration, and the sensation of being unable to calm down.

People with anxiety disorders frequently have norepinephrine systems that do not function properly. In response to even the most minor things, they may produce an excessive amount of that chemical and then experience difficulties removing it from their bodies when the stressor is gone. A few kinds of beta-blockers, the group of drugs that is aimed at cutting down anxiety, achieve this goal by preventing norepinephrine from sending signals to the rest of the body.

Dopamine: The Motivation Molecule

Dopamine is a celebrated player in the role of the pleasure and reward system, but it is also a significant contributor to anxiety. This neurotransmitter oscillates between enhancing behavior and facilitating the experience of pleasure and satisfaction. One of the ways anxieties can be turned up is through dopamine dysregulation.

Too little dopamine can cause anhedonia, which is the inability to derive pleasure from things, which is usually anxiety's most frequent companion. Life, in this case, is like rough terrain: if we cannot derive pleasure and a sense of reward from the things we used to like, the world becomes threatening and uncertain; thus, we get stuck in an anxiety cycle.

On the contrary, there are some cases when anxious people might have quite dopamine responses to the situations that might bring them the possible rewards, and therefore go to the point of addiction to that behavior, as they are constantly looking for ways to alleviate the symptoms of their anxiety. Hence, this is the link between anxiety disorders and the occurrence of substance addiction.

Cortisol: The Stress Hormone

Cortisol plays a vital role in the human anxiety system. It is through the adrenal glands that cortisol is produced. The hormone is released as part of the body's response to stress, and this signal triggers the rapid gathering of energy resources to combat the threat.

In the short term, the hormone cortisol has a beneficial effect on the body, helping us remain alert during challenging situations. Nevertheless, its continuous high level is very often found among people with anxiety disorders, and this condition can be dangerous both for physical and mental health.

High cortisol levels can lead to a shrinkage of the hippocampus, a part of the brain. This, in turn, can affect memory and lead to confusion about whether the threat is real. Besides these effects, cortisol influences the immune system, the sleep cycle, and the metabolism. Hence, chronic anxiety becomes a domino effect of physical health problems.

The Body's Response: From Brain to Biology

The anxiety system is not limited to the brain; instead, it involves communication throughout the entire body. The brain is the command processor that detects threats and initiates a complex physiological response, which is the mechanism for survival. It is only by knowing these bodily changes that one can realize that anxiety is very tough physically and that it affects our health.

The Autonomic Nervous System: Automatic Responses

The autonomic nervous system (ANS) controls automatic physiological activities, including breathing, heart rate, digestion, and body temperature regulation.

It has two main parts: the sympathetic nervous system (our "gas pedal") and the parasympathetic nervous system (our "brake pedal"). This system was designed to assist the ancestors in fleeing from predators, and it excels at preparing the body for action. Within seconds after a threat is perceived, the sympathetic nervous system has the power to alter our entire physiology.

The parasympathetic nervous system, however, is the body system that calms the body and returns it to its normal state after stress or an emergency. Gradually, it decreases the heart rate, supports digestion, and thus indirectly helps the body to recover and repair itself. People who are suffering from chronic anxiety usually have the parasympathetic nervous system being less active for a long time. As a result, they find it very hard to unwind and recuperate from the stressful situation.

Cardiovascular Changes: Racing Heart and Beyond

One of the effects of anxiety, which is visible to the naked eye, is the influence that anxiety has on the cardiovascular system. As we become anxious, our heart rate increases, blood pressure elevates, and blood flow shifts to large muscle groups, diverting from organs that are less crucial for the body's immediate survival. The purpose of these changes is to get us ready for physical action.

An increase in heart rate during anxiety is part of a larger picture where the heart not only works harder but also changes its characteristics. The heart rhythm during anxiety is less regular, and the variability in the rate is not as high as it is during breathing. This lower heart rate variability is associated with an increased risk of cardiovascular diseases in the future.

Blood vessels also alleviate some of the anxiety symptoms by narrowing some areas and expanding others. The blood directed toward the digestive system is diverted to the muscles we use for movement, which is why we might feel like vomiting or lose our appetite when anxious. Simultaneously, blood flow to the brain increases to quicken decision-making and concentration.

Respiratory Changes: The Breath-Anxiety Connection

Anxiety significantly affects the way you breathe. The usual slow and deep breathing when you are calm turns into fast and short breaths coming from the chest, rather than the diaphragm. While the body may quickly obtain more oxygen, the other physiological changes that accompany this can heighten anxiety.

Rapid breathing can lead to a decline in blood carbon dioxide levels, a condition known as hypocapnia. It thus changes the blood pH, and the accompanying symptoms are dizziness, tingling in the hands and feet, and feelings of unreality or detachment. The symptoms may be terrifying and, therefore, may increase the anxiety that the person has, thus establishing a vicious cycle.

Directionality of the breath-anxiety connection is two-way. Anxiety impinges on breathing patterns, and on the other hand, the impact of breathing patterns on the anxiety level is also present. This is the reason why breathing exercises are considered to be such an essential part of the anxiety management practice.

Muscular Responses: Tension and Tremor

The development of anxiety will eventually lead to enormous changes in the tension and activity of muscles. The muscles throughout the body become tense to the point where one may experience a headache, back pain, and a general feeling of physical discomfort. This muscle tension is usually very pronounced in people with anxiety disorders, and thus, they suffer from pain and fatigue for a long time.

There are some who, in that case, also get the shaking or the tremor that usually comes with anxiety. This is because the nervous system equips muscles for action, allowing small, rapid contractions to occur. The shaking may cause a person to feel embarrassed, but it is just one of the anxiety responses, and it usually goes away when anxiety is relieved.

Digestive System: The Gut-Brain Connection

The digestive system undergoes significant changes due to anxiety, providing an excellent example of the gut-brain connection. When a person is in danger, eating and digesting are not considered necessary. Consequently, anxiety leads to changes in appetite and bowel movements, stomach aches, and nausea.

The gut is the place where the enteric nervous system has more neurons than the spinal cord. The so-called "second brain" is always in contact with the brain in our head via the vagus nerve and other routes. The gut-brain connection is one of the reasons why we might feel anxiety as "butterflies" in our stomach or why anxiety disorders that are there for a long time are often linked with digestive problems.

Besides, the gut is filled with bacteria in the quadrillions that create neurotransmitters and other substances that can change the mood and cause anxiety. The gastrointestinal microbiome can adjust to stress, diet, and medications, making it a new area where anxiety can impact physical health.

The Mind-Body Loop: How Thoughts and Biology Interact

One of the most impressive points about anxiety is that our thoughts and physical symptoms are connected through intricate feedback loops. Our brains constantly supervise our body's condition, and alterations in our physiology can strongly influence our thoughts and moods. Realizing these mind-body loops is vital to forming the right anxiety treatment plans.

Bottom-Up Processing: When the Body Leads

There are times when the feeling of anxiety is due to physical sensations without any thoughts. Before you realize that you are anxious, you may notice an increase in heart rate, feel a slight dizziness, or experience muscle tension. This bottom-up processing occurs when your brain recognizes regular physical changes as danger signals.

If you have experienced a panic attack in your past, then your brain might become very vigilant to an involuntary change in your breathing or your heartbeat. One relatively small change in the pressure in your heart because of caffeine, sport, or even a change from sitting to standing might be perceived as the return of the panic attack, and only then can the whole anxiety be triggered.

Due to all these reasons, individuals suffering from anxiety disorders tend to develop an extreme attention to the minor bodily changes. It is recognized as interoceptive sensitivity. Some levels of body awareness are not harmful, though. Yet, a person who finds himself totally concentrated on his internal sensations may become a victim of chronic hypervigilance that, in turn, contributes to the maintenance of anxiety.

Top-Down Processing: When Thoughts Drive Physical Responses

Furthermore, anxiety is usually caused by thinking first, and then it spreads like a contagion to the body. Whether worrying about a future event, ruminating on a past mistake, or catastrophizing about one of the potential outcomes, these mental processes can trigger the same physiological reactions as real threats.

It's incredibly complex how our brains come up with negative futures. But our nervous system reacts with the same intensity as if the dreadful event is really taking place. So, the similarity between the scaring of a horror movie or a vividly remembered nightmare lies in the fact that they cause real physical symptoms of fear.

One example of mind-power-to-physiology is as strong as the placebo effect and psychosomatic symptoms. Our assumptions and projections can instantly alter our biological functions, highlighting a strong link between the brain and the body.

The Anxiety Spiral: Amplification Through Feedback

The feedback loop between thoughts and physical sensations is probably the most crucial idea when it comes to comprehending anxiety. This loop can go both ways and can, very quickly, escalate minor worries to entire anxiety episodes.

Usually, the anxiety spiral is triggered either by an alarming thought or some strange body sensation. In the case when it would begin with an idea ("What if I make a fool out of myself during the presentation?"), It would then provoke bodily symptoms such as hyperventilation. The brain then observes these physical changes and takes them as evidence that the worry is real; hence, more anxious thoughts and symptoms follow.

If the unraveling of the loop occurs in the body (for instance, discovering your heart rate has only increased), then perhaps you would think something like "What is the reason my heart is ticking so fast? Am I having a heart attack?" This statement will then lead to more physical symptoms, thereby initiating an identical amplifying process.

Firstly, it is essential to understand that the spiral effect is significant because it reveals several ways in which an intervention can be beneficial. You can break down the cycle by dealing with the thoughts (using cognitive therapy), the symptoms (through relaxation or breathing exercises), or the recognition process that links them.

Neuroplasticity: The Brain's Ability to Change

The most significant revelation of neuroscience is the discovery of neuroplasticity, which refers to the brain's capacity to restructure and form new connections throughout the entire lifespan. Accordingly, the changes that the brain presents in anxiety disorders are not permanent. However, we can actually alter our brain circuits to a less anxious state with the right treatments.

Every time we work on a different reaction to fear, it involves a relaxation method, a new thought pattern about a situation, or a behavioral change, we "create" strengthened neural pathways for a calm and resilient state. After many such experiences, these new pathways can supersede those old anxiety ones.

This change requires patience and is dependent on the number of repetitions. The time required for patterns of anxiety to be deeply ingrained is just like the time needed for new, healthier patterns to be established. Yet, the brain's innate plasticity gives change a chance even if a person has been dealing with anxiety for a very long time.

Genetic and Environmental Influences

Anxiety is a complex interaction between a person's genetic makeup and their life experiences that gives rise to it. One of the possible explanations for the differing susceptibilities to anxiety among people and the wide range of anxiety types is the understanding of these factors.

Genetic Contributions: The Anxiety Blueprint

Studies indicate that the genetic component of anxiety disorders is quite substantial, with the part of the condition that is inherited estimated to be from 30% to 60% depending on the disorder. This suggests that the risk of anxiety in us, which is passed down genetically from our parents, however, there is mutual consent that genetics doesn't exclusively rule, as the environment is just as influential and significant.

It is not that we inherit anxiety; instead, we receive genes that are competent in neurotransmitter function, stress reactivity, and temperament. As an illustration, some people receive genes that change the way serotonin or GABA functions, thus making them that much more vulnerable to anxiety if they undergo stress. While others might have genes that determine how fast their bodies remove stress hormones.

Temperament, which is mostly inherited, also affects the risk of anxiety. Some children, due to their highly responsive nervous systems, are so sensitive to their environment that even slight stimulation can trigger a fear reaction when encountering a new situation. The characteristic of a temperamental child, sometimes labeled as behavioral inhibition, refers to the most significant factor of the following anxiety disorders in the course of the child's development.

Environmental Triggers: Life Experiences That Shape Us

The experiences we have, especially those in our early life, can either activate or mitigate our genetic vulnerabilities. Recognizing these environmental factors helps clarify why anxiety occurs at certain ages and why symptoms arise after a particular event.

Early childhood experiences are highly significant due to the development of the brain. Kids who have undergone trauma, neglect, or continuous stress may develop nervous systems that are extremely vigilant. At times, these types of experiences may have them stay on high alert for their whole lives. What appear to be insignificant incidents, such as having anxious parents, may be a source of anxiety in a child.

Even so, the impact of the environment on mental health is still an issue beyond childhood. Anxiety among the vulnerable can be brought about by life changes and transitions, long-lasting stressors, sad occurrences, and even good things. What really matters is often not the event itself, but how it fits in with our existing weaknesses and coping abilities.

Epigenetics: The Impact of the Environment on Gene Expression
One of the most intriguing discoveries about anxiety that has come to light is the field of epigenetics, which refers to the study of how non-genetic factors can impact gene expression without altering the base sequence of DNA. This grounds the argument on how nature can be reflected in the long term in our biology, and, in some cases, these changes can be passed down from one generation to another.

First of all, chronic stress, along with traumatic events, may lead to DNA modifications that regulate the expression of anxiety-related genes. These epigenetic alterations may amplify an individual's sensitivity to subsequent stressors and persist for a long time after the original stressor has resolved.

At the same time, some epigenetic changes may be reversed if an individual undergoes positive experiences and receives the proper treatment. This suggests that though our genes are fixed, we can still influence how they are expressed through our decisions and experiences.

The Modern Anxiety Epidemic
The anxiety circuit that served our ancestors well for the last million years is now struggling to cope with the challenges of the modern world. The explanation of the interconnection between contemporary life and our evolutionary biology, which helps us understand the spread of anxiety disorders and offers clues for possible cures, is the central theme of this chapter.

The Mismatch Problem

Our minds and bodies were developed for conditions that bear little similarity to those we are living in now. The most common types of danger throughout history were only immediate, physical, and could be solved by taking action. A predator either seized you or you took flight; you either got food or starved; social disputes were settled face-to-face within small, homogenous communities.

The threats we face today are often undefined, complex, and long-lasting. We are constantly worried about losing our jobs, global warming, the way people treat us online, and a range of other issues. These concerns only make us feel more anxious, but we don't feel ready to handle them. Our brains are not able to separate or to calculate what is dangerous in the modern world, so they still react to these issues as if they were real killing instances, hence the chronic activation of organ systems that were created for quick and extreme situations.

One more cause of anxiety is technology and information overload. The information-rich modern world puts a lot of pressure on people, leading to anxiety. We are constantly being overwhelmed by information about global threats, the lives of people around the world as shared on social media, and the need to make decisions about almost everything without considering the consequences.

The human brain developed in an environment where humans had access to news only about what was happening in their immediate surroundings and within a small community. Today, this information overload is akin to a constant alarm ringing for our threat detection systems, putting them in an active mode, always on the lookout for hidden dangers in the vast ocean of data.

Social media is one of the most popular reasons for anxiety, and there are several dissimilar mechanisms through which it happens, which are: social comparison, fear of missing out, cyberbullying, and the addictive intermittent reinforcement of likes and comments. Since the events that others mostly want us to see in their lives are merely the opinions of lucky people about their own lives, we begin to doubt what we have, as it seems overshadowed by what others have.

The world is changing. One central area that could significantly impact human behavior is the global adoption of the latest technology. Nearly all parts of the world, including the remotest villages, are connected with various advanced technologies. A characteristic of these technologies is that they are evolving rapidly and continually improving. The emergence of new technologies indicates the loss of old ones. For instance, with the desire to have smart homes, people are no longer buying and using ordinary electric appliances. Our contemporary generation of young people is primarily drawn to the internet world and is not fond of reading books.

Almost all the advantages of the modern lifestyle have some negative aspects, such as the use of cars that cause pollution; however, people still cannot do without cars. We all love technological devices because of their convenience, but have we ever considered that they could be the end of our existence?

The disappearance of these natural regulators for our body has triggered an ideal setting for the rise of anxiety. The situation without the necessary amount of daily physical exercises to get rid of stress hormones, proper sleep to enable the brain to regain its functions, and last but not least, social interactions, which are the most important because of the safety and the support they provide, will result in our anxiety systems becoming rather chronically dysregulated.

Implications for Treatment and Management

Treating the anxiety disorder and knowing which treatment will work takes learning anxiety science. Instead of imagining anxiety as an attribute of a person's character that he lacks or that he is weak, we can understand it as a complex biological process that reacts to administered interventions.

Biological Interventions

One of the most effective justifications for those individuals extremely disturbed by anxiety is pharmacological therapy, which aids in targeting the central nervous system with specific neurotransmitters.

The SSRI and SNRI medications assist in stabilizing serotonin and norepinephrine systems, whereas the administration of benzodiazepines allows for a quick rescue as it strengthens the GABA functions. Nevertheless, taking medication as the only form of relief is indispensable and is more efficient if done concurrently with other methods.

Psychological Interventions

Among other methods, the psychological approach, together with cognitive-behavioral therapy (CBT), demonstrates the power of changing brain function through learning new ways of thinking and behaving. We are reprogramming the brain to become a new, peaceful, and resilient one by stimulating the neural pathways strengthened by calm and weakening those weakened by anxiety. Brain changes found in psychotherapy are mostly the same as those that appear with medication treatment.

Lifestyle Interventions

As anxiety affects the whole body, lifestyle changes that focus on physical health can be surprisingly powerful. Regular exercise, sufficient sleep, good nutrition, stress management, and social connection all significantly boost the bodily systems involved in anxiety.

Mind-Body Approaches

The methods that focus on the mind-body connection, such as meditation, yoga, breathing exercises, and progressive muscle relaxation, are highly effective as they interrupt the feedback loops that perpetuate anxiety. These methods provide people with knowledge of the relationship between thoughts and the body, as well as the skills to change both.

Anxiety science reveals that the whole thing humans often experience is not weakness or failure but rather the result of the complex interaction of ancient biological systems and new environmental challenges. By comprehending how our brains and bodies react to the dangers we feel, we can come up with kinder and more efficient ways of dealing with anxiety and helping those who have a hard time.

Mapping Your Triggers and Patterns

Becoming Your Own Detective

Understanding your anxiety calls for investigation. Like a skillful detective, you will have to collect evidence, find trends, and link the pieces together to form a picture of your singular anxiety case. This process of identifying your triggers and patterns is essential to marshalling the management strategies effectively because anxiety seldom appears out of the blue. Commonly, some factors can be identified that either trigger anxiety or make one more vulnerable to it.

Think of the life of Patricia. She was feeling for a long time that her anxiety was both unpredictable and overpowering. She had some good days, but others were dominated by her worries and the resulting physical tension. Eventually, by logging her experiences, she found out that her anxiety was always elevated on Sunday evenings, before having to return to work the next morning. She also found that during times when she had not engaged in any physical activity for several days. Recognizing this pattern helped her plan for vulnerable times and implement preventive measures.

Your aim in recognizing your triggers and setting patterns is not to escape entirely from anxiety-provoking situations because that would be unhealthy as well. The aim, however, is to build awareness that will enable you to present a better response when anxiety arises and to be well-informed while navigating difficult situations.

Understanding Triggers vs. Vulnerabilities

It is of utmost importance to figure out the differences between vulnerabilities and triggers before embarking on the mapping journey. Triggers are quite narrowly defined events, situations, or stimuli that cause the anxiety reaction to be activated directly. They may be external (e.g., a crowded place or a complicated conversation) or internal (e.g., physical changes or specific thoughts). Usually, the triggers are pretty stable in that they almost always give rise to anxiety upon encountering them.

Vulnerabilities, conversely, are elements that expose a person to an anxiety attack, but they do not have a direct link to causing it. They include factors such as sleep deprivation, hormonal changes, stress levels, physical health, and emotional state. When the vulnerabilities are at their top, the chances are that you will get anxious even in those situations that usually don't bother you, and may become nervous due to triggers.

Imagine the vulnerabilities as the backdrop against which the triggers exist. Giving a public speech, for instance, might be under your control if you are rested, healthy, and self-assured. However, the very same event can make you have an intense anxiety attack if you are sleep-deprived, fighting a cold, and relationship stress is bothering you.

The Anxiety Mapping Process

If you want to map anxiety patterns, it's best to take it step-by-step, carefully, and over an extended period. Though you might be tempted to assume that you are already aware of your triggers and that the patterns are apparent, the reality is that the tracking often conveys unexpected insights. People frequently find their anxiety to be more intraclass than initially thought, or they come up with very faint triggers that were unnoticed before.

The act of mapping entails numerous functions: the first is tracking anxiety episodes, followed by identifying triggers, recognizing vulnerabilities, noticing patterns, and finally, understanding your unique anxiety signature. Every function adds helpful information to the global scene.

Creating Your Anxiety Log

An anxiety log is a detailed account of your anxiety moments. At first, one may feel that this is a very monotonous task; however, with the insights extracted from tracking, the development of specific management strategies becomes possible. Your log does not have to be complex. A consistent and straightforward tracking system is more useful than an elaborate one, as it is less likely to require maintenance.

At least, your anxiety journal should have the time and date when you were anxious, the energy level of the anxiety episode (maybe on a scale of 1-10), the condition you were in, what you thought caused the anxiety, physical symptoms that you felt, thoughts that occurred to you, and what you did to calm down. You can also track your sleep quality, stress levels, and physical condition. Any of these factors may impact your anxiety.

An example of an entry may be: "Tuesday, 3 PM, intensity 7/10. Waiting for job interview results. Triggered by checking email and seeing a message from HR. Physical symptoms: racing heart, sweaty palms, tight chest. Thoughts: 'They're going to reject me,' 'I'm not qualified for this job,' 'I'll never find work.' Response: Called my sister for reassurance, paced around the house."

One important thing is to be honest, and you should also be consistent in your tracking. Record both high and low anxiety days. The contrast can be as informative as the anxiety episodes themselves. Be more specific about the situations and triggers you experienced, rather than using vague descriptions. "Felt anxious at work" is less helpful than "Felt anxious during team meeting when asked to present my project status."

Identifying External Triggers

External triggers are locations, things, or events that cause negative feelings in you. For example, the triggers might be giving presentations or taking more obvious tests, whereas sounds, smells, or visual cues can be pretty subtle triggers. Typically, external triggers can be categorized into the following areas: social situations, work or academic challenges, medical appointments, financial discussions, crowded spaces, driving, flying, and conflict situations.

Some of the external triggers that cause anxiety are different from others in nature. For instance, the occurrence of a job interview can be a trigger of anxiety, specifically for you. However, you can still be calm and feel at ease in other evaluative situations. Or you can be so anxious that you will be generally triggered in any case where you feel judged or evaluated.

Also, physical environments could be the main reason for people's anxiety. While some individuals may become anxious in tight spaces, others may be triggered by large spaces or high places. Sensory triggers could be anything, such as a loud noise, a very bright light, a strong-smelling substance, or a particular texture of the surface. Most of the time, these sensory triggers can be connected to past experiences or represent some threat to them.

Another type of trigger to consider is time-based triggers. In fact, many people experience heightened anxiety at particular times during the day, on certain days of the week, and even at certain seasons of the year. For instance, the feeling of anxiety on Sunday evening is quite common among those who dread starting their week at work on Mondays. Additionally, the exact day on which a significant incident occurred can also be a trigger.

Identifying Internal Triggers

Internal triggers refer to those that originate from within you, both physically and mentally. They can be physical sensations, thoughts, emotions, or memories. For example, physical sensations such as rapid heart rate, dizziness, and stomach upset can be triggers of anxiety in the case of people who have had a panic attack. As a result, there is this feedback loop when the physical sensations that are pretty normal are viewed as signs that danger is near, which causes the anxiety to grow, together with the physical symptoms.

Thoughts and pictures that come to one's mind can be powerful triggers. Thinking of the worst-case scenario of what could happen, recollections of the times when one had difficulties, or even sudden what-if situations are just a few of the things that can cause the body's anxiety reaction. At times, these thoughts are your conscious and deliberate ones, but mostly, they are automatic, and you barely notice them.

Theories related to emotions can also be the reason for the anxiety. Overwhelmed feelings, sadness, frustration, and even excitement can raise the openness to anxiety. Individuals can become anxious if they are angry, perhaps because the feeling of anger is overwhelming or because they feel unworthy of it.

Others get anxious when they become happy, probably due to the fear that the good things will not last. Sleep and nightmares are phenomena that can be the internal triggers of anxiety. First, a nightmare can lead to an anxiety episode that can still be present the next day. Some people feel anxious as soon as they wake up, before the process of conscious thought begins. The reason for this might lie in the content of their dreams or the sleep cycle.

Vulnerability factors are those aspects that do not cause anxiety but make the individual more prone to it. These factors cause situations in which the occurrence of anxiety becomes most likely when meeting the triggers. Sleep quality is the most crucial vulnerability factor. Sleep deprivation impairs emotional regulation, stress hormone levels, and cognitive functioning in a manner that increases anxiety vulnerability. Even a little sleep debt can make you more reactive to stressors and less capable of handling difficult situations.

Your physical health status has a significant influence on anxiety vulnerability. Illness, pain, hormonal changes, medication side effects, and substance use are some of the things that can lower your anxiety threshold. Caffeine, alcohol, and certain medicines that are taken can make anxiety symptoms get worse. Changes in your blood sugar levels that result from the way you eat can also help make you more prone to anxiety.

Stress levels give rise to cumulative vulnerability. For instance, if you were to handle multiple stressors at the same time, then the total you get from your stress load will increase your anxiety levels towards any other additional challenges. Hence, it is understandable why during difficult periods, anxiety appears to be much worse, and your coping resources are already overstretched.

Relationship conflict, which in turn leads to anxiety vulnerability, is one of the relationship principles that has a significant impact on anxiety vulnerability. On top of that, social isolation and relationship insecurity can be the source of such stress that eventually will make you vulnerable to anxiety triggers. On the other hand, the presence of strong social support can serve as a shield that lessens the anxiety vulnerability.

Predictable time patterns are what we call the anxiety of many people. Mornings may bring worry right after waking, afternoons will feature an unexplained decline in energy, and soothing worry sessions can be practiced in the evening. Such patterns may be linked to natural bodily processes, such as circadian rhythms, fluctuations in blood sugar, the effects of caffeine, or stressors associated with daily activities.

Work and school schedules are the most common reasons for weekly patterns. The most common phenomena are Monday anxiety, midweek stress peaks, and Sunday evening anticipatory anxiety. These timings might be connected to workload cycles, social commitments, or the transition between weekends and weekdays.

Hormones may influence monthly cycles, and this is particularly true for women. The majority of females recognize that anxiety gets intensified at particular points of their menstrual cycle, mainly in the week that precedes menstruation. This can result from hormonal changes, physical discomfort, or simply being more sensitive to stressors.

Seasonal changes are also a point that should not be ignored. Anxiety levels of some people rise during dark months (which might be closely connected to Seasonal Affective Disorder). In contrast, some individuals find it more challenging to cope with high-stress moments, such as holidays or the beginning of the school year.

The Anxiety Spiral

Generally speaking, the anxiety spiral refers to the scenario wherein a trigger is the most likely point to start the whole chain reaction of anxiety. Once the trigger is there, the victim's threat detection system gets automatically activated. It can be either an external or an internal line of thought or a feeling. Your body reacts with initial changes in physical conditions, such as a rapid heart rate, gentle muscle tension, or altered breathing patterns.

In case these changes become visible and are taken as dangerous, they produce secondary anxiety. Anxiety caused by the issue of anxiety symptoms themselves. This explanation describes how feelings now intensify on the physical level, making the symptoms more observable. From this point, these symptoms are regarded as the most critical signs of threat. This is how the consequences can go one after another in a chain reaction, thereby leading very quickly to high anxiety or panic.

Some people first discover physical symptoms, while others recognize the occurrence of anxiety thoughts or changes in behavior. Learning to identify your personal early warning signs enables you to practice coping skills before the anxiety level gets so high that you cannot control it.

Behavioral Patterns

Notice the typical way that you react to an anxiety situation. Do you look for comfort from others, stay away from the situation that caused the anxiety, do something that takes your mind off the problem, or try to go on as usual even though you are not feeling well? Recognizing your behavior patterns is very important since some reactions, like avoidance, can keep or increase anxiety over time, whereas others, like gradual exposure, can lower it.

Safety behaviors are just minor avoidance strategies that people use to handle anxiety in a tricky situation. For example, this can refer to not making eye contact during a conversation or always standing near the exit in a crowded room. Though safety behaviors may give you a short comfort time, they can make you unable to learn that you can handle anxiety and that the feared outcomes don't happen most of the time.

In addition to the above, reassurance-seeking is a typical manifestation of a behavioral pattern. It may involve repeatedly asking someone the same question, seeking a specific answer that assures everything will be fine, reading information online, or checking for signs of problems to confirm your thoughts. Similar to safety behaviors, reassurance-seeking offers brief relief but can become habitual and, in this way, lead to an increase in anxiety with time.

Cognitive Patterns

The way you think significantly affects the development and continuation of anxiety. The typical cognitive patterns that anxiety is accompanied by are catastrophizing, such as seeing things only in the worst light, all-or-nothing thinking, such as seeing situations as totally good or horrible, mind-reading, such as assuming that you know what others are thinking, fortune-telling, such as predicting only the adverse future events, and downplaying your ability to cope with difficulties.

These are the thought processes that usually turn into your fixed, go-to reactions in case of anxiety and seem completely correct as well. Apart from this, they often involve distortions that make the situations appear more threatening than they actually are; recognizing these patterns is the first step in shifting one's thinking to more balanced and helpful perspectives.

Some people are so focused on thinking through problems that they become anxious about overlooking a single negative outcome when planning for everything else. This kind of behavior can sometimes be beneficial, but more often than not, it ends up being just a tedious and unproductive rumination that heightens rather than lessens anxiety.

The Role of Perfectionism

Perfectionism, on the one hand, is a significant cause of anxiety in the lives of people, and on the other hand, it acts as a factor that forever keeps the fire of anxiety burning for them. The perfectionistic point of view, which holds that a single mistake will lead to catastrophe, that everything less than perfect will be considered a failure, and that others expect absolute perfection from us, can result in an uptight state of never-ending anxiety about one's performance and being assessed.

Most of the time, perfectionism ends up as procrastination (fear of an imperfect result is the main reason for task putting off), over-preparation (more than the necessary time is spent on doing the task), or paralysis (due to the fear of mistakes, one is not able to start or finish the task). Anxiety about anxiety is another problem that perfectionism can also cause, as those with perfectionistic traits may be very self-critical and think that they are at fault for anxiety symptoms, maybe because of them and not because of any outside source.

Talking about perfectionism in the context of you and your personality can be a significant step in figuring out the situations that bother you and your anxiety patterns. Once you identify the perfectionistic tendencies and decide to work with them, then you are halfway to anxiety management in a way.

Social and Interpersonal Patterns

One of the frequent instances in which anxiety is manifested is in social relations. It will be beneficial for you to know what the interpersonal situations are with the people who may trigger your anxiety. For example, you can find that the feeling of anxiety is much higher when you are in a specific type of person's company, i.e., authority figures, attractive individuals, or people who remind you of someone from your past. Moreover, specific social situations, such as groups vs. one-on-one interactions, or formal vs. casual settings, may result in anxiety. Additionally, you may feel nervous due to specific social dynamics, such as conflict, evaluation, or competition.

Additionally, it is also essential to note your communication pattern. An anxious person may not necessarily behave the same way as the person next to them in the same situation. Some people become quiet and withdrawn, while others become talkative or agitated. Some seek connection and support, while others isolate themselves. When you make an effort to understand the changes, you will be able to express your needs clearly and request the corresponding support.

Family and Historical Patterns

There are times when you can detect similar patterns of anxiety in your family members, and at other times, you can tell that past experiences are still affecting your present reactions.

Experiences in childhood with safety, predictability, and emotional support will influence anxiety greatly in the adult stage. In case you were brought up in an environment that was not predictable, you may be on the lookout for danger or change coming at any time. Experiencing criticism or rejection may lead you to become very sensitive to social evaluation.

Traumatic experiences can lead to the formation of specific anxiety trigger patterns. Instances that bring up memories of previous traumas, whether you are aware of it or not, can result in the activation of anxiety symptoms that may appear to be out of proportion regarding the present situation, but are completely logical when viewed as a part of your history.

Cultural and Contextual Factors

How you look at the world, your money situation, and life conditions are the main factors that shape your anxiety pattern. The cultural issues about feeling, individual vs. group responsibility, and what is considered correct behavior may have an impact not only on the anxiety triggers but also on the coping response.

Discrimination, economic problems, and political instability are some of the societal factors that can lead to the development of anxiety. The factors you are talking about may not be the leading cause of anxiety; however, they set a stressful and uncertain environment from which anxiety may likely emanate.

Using Technology for Tracking

Many people can quite easily and comfortably use paper logs to monitor anxiety. Nonetheless, technology may be more effective in the long-term tracking of anxiety. Smartphones are equipped with mood and anxiety tracking apps that can make the task easier, not only by allowing quick data entry but also by providing a graphical view of your progress over time, as well as frequently reminding you to track your progress.

Moreover, if you wear devices that continuously track your heart rate, sleep quality, and physical activity, you can obtain the necessary objective data about the physical factors affecting your anxiety. In short, the data obtained from these devices is beneficial in revealing new anxiety patterns that you may have missed without these tools.

Just take it easy and don't allow yourself to become addicted to technology or extreme preoccupation with tracking. It is not about becoming yet more anxious but rather about having easy access to information that provides relief.

Analyzing Your Patterns

Once you have been processing tracking data for a few weeks, it is advisable to step back, review your data, and draw inferences. You may be astonished by what you uncover. You may find out that your anxiety is less erratic than you supposed or even identify triggers that were not manifested to you before.

Compare the different factors and see which correlate. Does your anxiety reach its peak level during specific weather patterns? Are there certain stressors that, when combined, always lead to anxiety? Do the effectiveness of particular coping strategies fluctuate depending on the situation?

Don't hope to discover evident and straightforward patterns right away. Anxiety is quite tricky, and the patterns may be very faint or complicated. Occasionally, the pattern appears to be absent. Anxiety looks as if it is random and baffling. This knowledge is also very valuable, as it insinuates that the factors of vulnerability might be more important than the specific triggers for your anxiety management.

Common Pattern Categories

Even though everyone's anxiety patterns differ, some categories may help sort out the observations you make. Some people have situational anxiety as the main direction of their anxiety. They are anxious only when the particular context or event occurs. Others are characterized by more generalized patterns of anxiety where such a sort of emotion can happen in different situations; however, it follows the same internal pattern.

Some people have cognitive-behavioral anxiety as the primary source of reactive anxiety. They tend to exhibit anxiety symptoms due to external stressors. On the other hand, there are more anticipatory types of anxiety. They feel anxious due to the anticipation of future stressors. Besides, there are still some people who derive both reactive and anticipatory anxiety patterns from the same source.

Many people experience time-of-day patterns of anxiety that become very consistent. In such cases, the situation can be linked with blood sugar cycles, caffeine effects, circadian rhythms, or even small, predictable daily stressors.

Creating Your Personal Anxiety Profile

By examining your symptoms and doing a pattern study, you will be able to compile a personal anxiety profile, which would be a detailed description of how anxiety appears in your one-of-a-kind life. This profile, for example, might involve the things that trigger your anxiety the most, the ways that anxiety is hinted at most often by you, factors that make you vulnerable to anxiety and need observation, extents of anxiety, and ways of both coping that work and those that don't, and high-risk times or places.

By having your anxiety profile, you can visualize your dependency on yourself and so come up with management strategies that will be more targeted. For example, if you know that Sunday nights are high-risk times, you can then plan activities that will be supportive to you during those times.

If you have discovered that poor sleep is a significant vulnerability factor, you can ensure you observe good sleep hygiene. In case you have identified that the most common thinking patterns which precede anxiety spikes are the ones called "overthinking" and "catastrophizing," you might thus engage yourself in the development of alternative thought patterns.

Working with Patterns vs. Fighting Them

When you discover your patterns, you are a step ahead, as you have control over how to use them. You may decide to change some patterns, while you plan to work on managing others.

Suppose anxiety before giving a speech at a formal event is a consistent pattern of behavior for you. In that case, you may choose to work on your speaking skills to reduce your anxiety gradually. On the other hand, you may focus on developing effective preparation routines and refining the coping strategies you will use before and during the presentation. It is not the primary purpose to remove all that causes anxiety from your life, as it is at the same time unachievable and not even preferable.

What remains, however, is the purpose of wisely reacting to your patterns by utilizing the resources of self-knowledge to master anxiety.

Sharing Your Insights

Think about passing your pattern discoveries to a few that you trust. Maybe friends, family, or even a mental health professional. They may have noticed similar patterns in other situations, which you may not be aware of. Moreover, they might be able to help you better when they understand your anxiety pattern. Psychotherapists will be able to assist in breaking down complex patterns and developing only a few effective intervention strategies. Additionally, they may help determine which patterns should be changed and which are merely normal fluctuations in human experience.

Evolving Patterns

Don't forget that the anxiety patterns can fluctuate with time. Some life changes, new worries, the ability to cope well, and personal development are all factors that can change your anxiety patterns. Take the time to continue learning and expanding your knowledge as you undergo personal growth and development. There are those patterns that at first glance seem not to change but are actually more flexible than you thought. Through the process of targeted intervention, even the earliest patterns can change. Besides that, some may even be deeply rooted in your personality or physical makeup and can be managed through adjustment rather than trying to be changed.

The Foundation for Growth

The knowledge of your triggers and patterns is the base upon which everything that follows in anxiety management is built. This self-awareness empowers you to decide when to challenge yourself and when to take it easy, when to ask for help and when to utilize your own resources, and which management strategies are most likely to be effective in a given situation.

In the next chapter, we will dive into the methods of physically dealing with anxiety. Having a pattern map as a reference, you will be able to use these tools not only randomly but also interchangeably and strategically, which will help you engage your self-knowledge to the greatest extent possible, thus allowing you to get the most out of these tools.

Physical Tools for Instant Relief

Your Body as an Ally

When anxiety hits, it seems like your body is just against you. Your heart pounds, your breath shortens, your muscles tighten, and you may also feel dizzy, sick, or as if you are disconnected from reality. At these times, your body seems to be the enemy. The source of unpleasant changes that, as it appears, confirms the worst fears you have about danger or losing control.

Still, the acknowledgment of anxiety's bodily side manifests a different reality. The body is, in fact, on your side and can be the most potent ally in the fight against anxiety. The very systems in our bodies that cause anxiety symptoms can be used to calm down, give comfort, and provide control. The chapter is centered on the presentation of physical techniques for anxiety that are practical and evidence-based, and they can be used to give relief right away.

One of the most attractive aspects of physical methods is their universal accessibility. Physical tools are always ready for use, with no need for special clothing or a designated space. Their direct interaction with the body's deep structures is akin to utilizing the body's own mechanisms to restore self-regulation and peace.

Understanding the Physical Foundation of Anxiety

It is still quite a challenge to accept this anxiety knowledge, but experiencing anxiety symptoms during which one's body is literally hijacked will call for a rethink of the fear tactic. Knowing what happens to your body during anxiety shifts the fear-anger dependence to curiosity, and from being a victim to becoming the master of the situation.

If your brain detects a situation as dangerous, whether it is real or merely an illusion, it will activate your body's sympathetic nervous system, also known as the body's accelerator.

This system prepares you for action by creating the following effects: speeding up the heart rate, elevating blood pressure, dilating the pupils, releasing stress hormones, and redirecting blood to the large muscles. Your breathing becomes rapid and shallow to provide more oxygen, and your muscles tighten in preparation for movement.

At the same time, the parasympathetic nervous system of the body, which is the brake system, remains inactive. This system is the polar opposite of the sympathetic nervous system, as it is responsible for processes such as sleep, digestion, calmness, and the general state of the body characterized by rest and relaxation. When anxiety is at its highest level, the parasympathetic system is at its lowest functional level.

The physical tools explained in this chapter either affect the body by lowering sympathetic activation or by improving the function of the parasympathetic system.

A few methods may even cause both effects simultaneously, moving towards a state of peace and control, thereby becoming more powerful.

The Power of Breath

Breathing is the most basic and effective tool for managing anxiety. It is the only bodily function that is both automatic and conscious at the same time, and thus it is' a perfect link between the body's anxiety mechanisms and the user's conscious control.

When you are anxious, your breathing is usually quick and shallow, and you tend to breathe primarily through the upper part of the chest. This type of breathing, although it is suitable for the immediate energetic response, can prolong anxiety if maintained for a long time. The shortness of breath that can be experienced may lead to feelings of faintness and a sense of detachment from the world. These feelings may further exacerbate anxiety, which in turn may perpetuate the cycle.

On the other hand, deep, slow, diaphragmatic breathing activates the parasympathetic nervous system, conveying to your brain the message that you are safe and secure. Such breathing literally alters the body's chemistry, resulting in lower levels of stress hormones and a calming, yet alert, state.

Basic Diaphragmatic Breathing

One of the most essential breathing characteristics is the use of the diaphragm muscle to draw air deeply into the lungs, rather than breathing shallowly through the chest muscles.

In the practice of diaphragmatic breathing, there should be one hand on your chest and one on your abdomen. After you have taken your breath slowly through your nose, allow your stomach to expand while the chest is kept still. The hand on your belly should be passing the hand on your chest in terms of the movement. When you slowly breathe out through your mouth, let your stomach fall naturally.

At first, this might seem very uncomfortable or even forced, especially if you are a habitual chest breather. Diaphragmatic breathing develops into a natural and automatic habit with practice. Most people feel that it is easier to do it when they are already relaxed, which then becomes more accessible during times of anxiety.

The 4-6-8 Technique

This technique is highly effective in alleviating panic within a short time. It is one of the most efficient methods, as evidenced by the numbers representing the seconds spent on each breathing phase.

Quietly breathe in through the nose for four counts, hold your breath for six counts, and then breathe out fully through the mouth for eight counts, producing a whoosh sound. Do this 3-4 times, or until you feel calm.

The extended exhale is key as it maximally activates the parasympathetic nervous system. Holding your breath allows for optimal oxygen-carbon dioxide exchange and gives you a sense of control over your body's responses.

Box Breathing

Square or box breathing is another name for a mind control technique used by military personnel, athletes, and first responders, which helps maintain a calm focus during challenging times. This method involves setting the same duration for each breathing phase.

Inhale for four counts, hold for four counts, exhale for four counts, hold empty for four counts. Repeat this pattern 4-8 times. You can adjust the length of the count based on your lung capacity and comfort.

Some people prefer three counts, others can comfortably do 6. Box breathing is beneficial in situations where you need to remain calm and focused. Still, anxiety is causing you to have trouble, for example, talking in front of people, taking a test, or having a difficult conversation.

Physiological Sighing

Brain research supports this method, which involves a specific double inhale immediately followed by a long exhale. It is a technique for quickly shutting off the nervous system, which is more effective for immediate anxiety relief than for gradual relief.

Mouth one typical nose inhale, and then immediately, on top of the first one, mouth a second, smaller one. With the double inhale, you fill up your lungs to the full capacity, even the small air sacs that are usually empty during stress breathing. Consequently, breathe out slowly and thoroughly with your mouth.

Just one or two physiological sighs can instantly change the nervous system state. This is a good technique for quick relief when you have very little time and cannot do a prolonged breath exercise.

Progressive Muscle Relaxation

Muscle torture is at the same time the result of anxiety and a factor that feeds it. In case you are overwhelmed, your muscles will tighten as a way of preparation for fight or flight. This tightness can become constant, escalating a loop of physical suffering that tells your brain that there is a problem, and thus, the cycle of anxiety continues.

Progressive Muscle Relaxation (PMR) helps dissolve tension by systematically tensing and then relaxing every muscle group in your body. This step-by-step guide enables you to distinguish between tensing and relaxing muscles and also provides control over muscle tension.

Basic PMR Technique

Be located in a spot that is both comfortable and peaceful. Beginning with your feet, intentionally contract each muscle group for 5-7 seconds, then release the tension and concentrate on the feeling of relaxation for 10-15 seconds before moving to the next muscle group.

Systematically work your way through your body: toes, feet, calves, thighs, buttocks, abdomen, hands, forearms, upper arms, shoulders, neck, face, and scalp. Full-time, 15-20 minutes are required for this process; however, even a short version concentrating on the big muscle groups can also be effective.

The central point is that you are showing the difference between tension and relaxation. When you initially tense the muscle groups, you can better recognize and feel the relaxation. Most people are surprised when they discover they have a significant amount of muscle tension, often without being aware of it.

Quick Muscle Release

If you are unable to perform a full PMR but still want to, quick muscle release is an option that can be targeted at areas where you typically experience tension. Tension can be found in the following spots:

Shoulders: Pull your shoulders up to your ears, hold for 5 seconds, then let them go and roll them back

Jaw: Clench your jaw muscles, keep for a while, then make your jaw slightly open

Hands: Make tight fists, keep them for a while, and then open your hands and shake them out

Face: Scrunch all your facial muscles together, keep for a while, and then relax and smooth your expression

These rapid releases from tension can be done at any place and give instant relief from physical stress that leads to anxiety.

Grounding Through the Senses

When anxiety is high, you might feel disconnected from your body or your environment. This phenomenon is called dissociation or derealization. Grounding techniques use your senses to reconnect you with the present moment and your physical reality.

The 5-4-3-2-1 Technique

This is a well-known grounding method that engages all five senses to help you return to the present moment. As you become that anxious, point out:

5 things you can see (look around and name specific objects)

4 things you can touch (feel different textures around you)

3 things you can hear (listen for both evident and subtle sounds)

2 things you can smell (notice scents in your environment)

1 thing you can taste (this might be subtle, like the taste in your mouth)

The way this technique works is to move the focus of your attention from internal anxiety symptoms to external reality. It's perfect for panic attacks or situations when you are swamped with anxious thoughts that you cannot get rid of.

Temperature Techniques

Temperature changes can drastically and quickly alter your nervous system state. Cold stimulation, in particular, is highly effective in interrupting anxiety spirals, as it activates the parasympathetic nervous system, which is closely linked to the vagus nerve.

Temperature techniques are straightforward and are as follows:

Splashing cold water on your face or wrists

Grabbing ice cubes with your hands and holding them

Going outside and feeling the cold air

Taking a cold shower (or just finishing a warm shower with cold water)

Placing a cold compress on your neck or forehead

The cold temperature produces an immediate body change that can cut through the anxiety symptoms when most other techniques do not work.

Texture and Touch

Sensual touch is the way to the very center of being, and it is thus very grounding. Carry small objects that feel nice to the touch in your pockets or your bag. Examples may include smooth stones, felted fabric, stress balls, or fidget toys. When anxiety gets the better of you, concentrate on touching these objects and feeling them.

Some people tend to resort to the help of self-massage when they suffer from an anxiety attack. The use of gentle pressure on the temples, neck, or hands can help relax the muscles and provide a comforting sense of touch. The essence of it all is that the pressure should be tight enough to feel soothing and soft enough not to cause pain.

Movement and Exercise

Movement is a very effective method to deal with anxiety as it is the one that closes the action loop that the nervous system activates in stressful situations. When your body is in the process of becoming ready for fighting or fleeing, movement will be your way of getting rid of the stress hormones and energy that have been mobilized by anxiety.

Immediate Movement Options

First of all, at the moment of panic, if you have space to move, why not consider these options:

Brisk walking, especially outdoors

Besides jumping jacks, doing other quick and straightforward calisthenics

Just playing your favorite song and dancing to that music only

Doing stretching exercises or practicing yoga

Do you experience shaking of your limbs (shaking your hands, arms, and legs)

Moving quickly up and down stairs

The main thing is to decide on the type of movement that will give you pleasure and will match your current mood. There are times when light movement is more suitable than vigorous one, especially if you are feeling too tired.

Yoga for Anxiety

Anxiety is one of the most significant contributors to depression, and the one thing that can heal the adverse effects of anxiety is yoga. However, the efficacy of yoga in self-help for anxiety is contingent upon the adoption of connected and mindful breathing during asana practice. The most common yoga poses for anxiety are:

Child's pose (knees on ground, sitting back on heels, arms extended forward)

Legs up the wall pose (lying on back with legs elevated against a wall)

Cat-cow stretches (on hands and knees, alternately arching and rounding the spine)

Forward fold (standing and folding forward over the legs)

Corpse pose (lying flat on back in complete relaxation)

These asanas not only promote calm activities, which are all parasympathetic nervous system responses, but also provide the practitioner with instant relief and long-term benefits in anxiety management.

Desk-based Movement

In case you are at work or some other place where you cannot move

Openly, you can still engage in some subtle exercises that will help you feel better. Ankle circles and calf raises under your desk, Shoulder blade squeezes, Neck rolls, Seated spinal twists, and Deep breathing with slight movement of the arms. Without drawing much attention, these movements can help you release body tension and bring some of the benefits of exercise to you.

Vagus Nerve Stimulation

The vagus nerve is the longest of the cranial nerves and makes up a large part of the parasympathetic nervous system. The vagus nerve stimulation can rapidly bring the body's calm reaction as well as lower the anxiety symptoms.

Humming and Singing

One of the ways that humming or singing can cause is the stimulation of the vagus nerve. You don't have to be a good singer—any vocal vibrations will suffice. Consider trying:

Humming your favorite tune

Singing in the shower or car

Making "om" sounds during meditation

Gargling with water

Laughing (even forced laughter creates beneficial vibrations)

Cold Water Face Immersion

When you splash cold water on your face or immerse it in cold water, you trigger the "dive response" that stimulates the vagus nerve and quickly calms the nervous system. This method is especially effective in severe anxiety or panic episodes.

Gentle Neck Massage

The vagus nerve is one of the things that goes through your neck, and a very gentle massage of the neck and throat area can help in the process. Use your circular motions and apply light pressure to both sides of your neck, avoiding direct pressure on the throat, which is why you must be careful when doing it.

The Power of Posture

Your physical posture has a significant impact on your emotional state through a phenomenon called embodied cognition. The concept that the body's position affects the mind. Anxiety is often accompanied by collapsed, defensive postures: shrunk shoulders, a rounded spine, and an inward-turned body position.

Power Posturing

Scientists have found that the confident and open postures, whether standing or sitting, can not only lower the secretion of the stress hormone but also raise feelings of power and tranquility. Examples of such postures are:

Being stately with the shoulders pulled back and hands on the hips

Keeping the back straight and chest open while seated

Throwing your arms up in a victory gesture

Using the space around you to expand rather than crowding yourself

These postures must be maintained for at least two minutes to trigger changes in the body's physiology. Although it may be a bit awkward at first, the biochemical effects are indeed very real and measurable.

Grounding Through Feet

The anxiety that makes you feel fragile is the one upon which you ought to put your feet firmly on the ground, mentally speaking. That is, whether you are standing or sitting:

Feel the ground with the balls of your feet and heels

Move your toes up and down inside your shoes

Move gently forward and backward to feel your weight on the ground

Visualize roots growing from your feet and going into the earth

Such a straightforward exercise can help you feel secure immediately and stay grounded.

Creating Your Physical Toolkit

No one will find every technique suitable for their personal skills or situation. The purpose is to try out several kinds of the same and to select those that are the closest to both your physical self and your given circumstances.

Situation-Specific Tools

Consider which techniques would be most effective in different settings:

At work: Breathing techniques, subtle movement, posture adjustments

At home: Full PMR, yoga, cold water techniques, vigorous movement

In social situations: Discrete breathing, grounding through senses, posture work

During panic: Physiological sighing, cold stimulation, grounding techniques

Intensity-Matched Interventions

Tailor the intervention to the anxiety intensity you have:

Mild anxiety: Simple breathing adjustments, posture corrections

Moderate anxiety: Full breathing techniques, muscle releases, movement

Severe anxiety: Intensive grounding, cold stimulation, vigorous movement

Preparation and Practice

Physical techniques are most effective when they are familiar and automatic. Practice using these tools when you are calm, so they will be easily accessible when anxiety arises. Also, consistent practice strengthens your confidence in your ability to control anxiety, which in turn can be a factor in the decrease of anxiety intensity.

Understanding Limitations

The limitations of physical techniques must be taken into account, despite their power. They can relieve the symptoms of anxiety and can play a significant role in anxiety spirals, but they are not at the root of the causes of anxiety. If you often use these techniques, it may be a sign that you need additional strategies and/or support.

Physical methods are likewise more successful when joined with alternative strategies. They can provide a sense of relief that can open the way for the use of mental strategies, lifestyle changes, or professional help.

Building Long-Term Physical Resilience

As an alternative to immediate relief techniques, building overall physical resilience will significantly reduce your anxiety. This is composed of regular exercise, sufficient sleep, a balanced diet, and effective stress management techniques. These four basic things establish a sounder, healthier way of coping with the complex situations in life.

Exercise is one of the elements that, if practiced regularly, will bring both instant management of anxiety and also contribute to the long-term anxiety remission process.

Physical activity decreases baseline anxiety levels, promotes good quality sleep, improves mood regulation, and enhances self-confidence in your body's potential.

Integration with Daily Life

The most effective way to utilize these techniques is to incorporate them into your daily routine, thereby making it the most successful approach. This could be a way to incorporate breathing exercises into your daily routine, such as doing them every morning before starting your day, moving around during breaks at work, or practicing progressive muscle relaxation before going to bed.

In other words, these tools can help you maintain your regular personal care routine, rather than being limited to emergency interventions. By regularly practicing, you keep your nervous system flexible, making these skills automatic so you'll be ready when the need arises.

The human body, along with its natural physiological changes, is a powerful anxiety management system waiting to be harnessed rather than opposed. Hence, the sense of power and command one gains from using these physical tools in the cognitive and emotional work of anxiety management is strengthened in those moments.

In the next chapter, we will examine how to manage your thoughts and understand the way your mind works, so that they align with these physical methods. The physical and the cognitive approaches form an open set of tools that allow you to work from different sides against anxiety.

Shaping Your Thoughts: Cognitive Strategies

The Mind's Role in Anxiety

Confusion, especially in the human mind, is manifested by the mind, which either amplifies or alleviates the distress, and the body likewise creates the bodily experience of anxiety. The association of thoughts and fear is intricate and a two-way traffic. Worrisome thoughts may precipitate physical symptoms, whereas the latter may evoke anxious thoughts. The approach to and dealing with your thinking, however, is the primary key to controlling anxiety in the long run.

Think of Evan's situation. When he notes his heartbeat speeding up during a meeting, his first thought is, "Everybody notices how nervous I am. They think I'm incapable." That thought, in turn, fuels more anxiety, which then makes his heart beat even faster, so he can see that his view that something is wrong is actually the case. While his co-worker Anita may also physically feel the same, her thought will be, "The good feeling is what has come about because of this presentation. My body is getting ready for the performance." Instead of anxiety, her explanation leads to getting self-confidence.

They still got the same effect of increased heart rate, but the difference is not in the physical sensation—it is in the way they each interpret and respond to it. It is one of the basic concepts behind cognitive treatment of anxiety that what makes us feel in a certain way is not the events themselves but the way we see them.

This, however, does not mean that anxiety is all in your head or that you can think yourself out of it. Anxiety is a combination of both real physical and emotional experiences, and thus, it is essential to recognize and take care of them. Nevertheless, the process of identifying and rearranging thought patterns shall have a considerable bearing on the duration and intensity of the anxiety that you face.

Understanding Thought Patterns in Anxiety

Moreover, anxiety can predictably distort your thoughts. The brain, which is designed to prioritize survival over accuracy, enters a mode where it focuses on detecting the threat rather than conducting a balanced evaluation. As a result, you begin to experience systematic biases in the way information is processed.

The cognitive distortions that you experience are not the result of character weaknesses or signs that the person is unreasonable; they are natural reactions of the body to a perceived threat, which was vital for the survival of our ancestors in dangerous situations. The problem is that these same patterns of thinking are capable of keeping and escalating anxiety in current conditions, which are different and where survival is not at risk.

Catastrophic Thinking

The most common cognitive distortion in anxiety might be, however, that of catastrophizing the worst-case scenarios and treating them as if they were to happen. When catastrophizing, your mind skips directly from the current concern to the most terrible possible outcomes, which it begins to imagine.

For example, a simple headache turns into a brain tumor. A slow response to a text message often means that the relationship is over. At work, an error can lead to termination, which could result in bankruptcy and ultimately leave us homeless. The brain often generates detailed disaster scenarios, with multiple adverse events unfolding one after another.

On its part, catastrophizing is still a function of the evolutionary process, as it promotes the development of skills necessary for facing a real danger. Nevertheless, if such a behavior were employed to deal with everyday stressors, it would essentially result in unnecessary suffering that would further incapacitate the individual from acting.

All-or-Nothing Thinking

Otherwise known as extreme thinking, this distortion is characterized by its characters viewing situations as either overly pessimistic or overly optimistic, with no other possibilities existing. Either you are a total success or a complete failure, totally safe or in great danger, perfectly ready or completely useless.

The pattern of thinking in extremes also escalates the person's anxiety, and it does so by taking away the detailed reality that nearly all situations are somewhere between the two ends of a range. Besides this, it also lays down such a standard for yourself, which is so high that it must end up in failure, and you will then release more anxiety through self-criticism.

Mind Reading

Anxious individuals often lead a life of assumptions, and thus they believe they can discern what is actually in other people's minds, and that they primarily think negatively about them. For example, you may see a person's neutral face as they being displeased with you, predict that the person who is silent in the conversation is angry, or think that others are concentrating on how bad you are, whilst they are probably worrying about their own lives.

Imagining what others might think is one of the causes of social anxiety as well as of problems in relationships, since a person reacts to what they assume is the other person's thoughts instead of what has been communicated. In addition, this hinders you from understanding what is really going on, which may result in a more positive or neutral outcome.

Fortune Telling

This concept involves foreseeing that only bad things will happen in the future with absolute confidence, even though there is no crystal ball to aid such predictions. Maybe you are pretty sure that you will fail a test, that you will be so ashamed at a party that you will want to disappear, or that you will be overcome by panic in a particular place.

Future telling is a process that makes us more anxious about non-existent adverse events than about actual events, which are sometimes less disturbing than anticipated. Moreover, this also becomes a self-perpetuating process when the foretellers cause the target to exhibit seclusion behaviors as a result of the prophecy.

Mental Filtering

When someone is anxious, their attention becomes intensely focused on only the threatening things, and they mentally disregard the rest of the world, which is neutral or positive. You may see one nasty comment among many lovely comments, concentrate on vanishing problems and overlook the growing signs of success, or recall awkward moments only to forget nice achievements.

This way of selective attention keeps anxiety going because it filters the evidence according to which it seems that anxious predictions and interpretations are being confirmed.

The Cognitive Model of Anxiety

Firstly, understanding the interaction between thoughts, feelings, and behaviors is crucial for effective cognitive intervention. The mental model suggests that situations lead to automatic thoughts, which cause feelings and physical sensations, thereby influencing behaviors. These behaviors then affect the problem, creating a feedback loop.

To illustrate the cycle:

Situation (job interview) → Automatic Thought ("I'll say something stupid") → Emotion (anxiety) → Physical Sensation (racing heart) → Behavior (avoiding eye contact, speaking quietly) → Consequence (interviewer seems unimpressed) → Reinforced Thought ("I knew I'd mess this up").

If someone were to stop any of the actions in this cycle, they would have a significant impact on the entire system. Cognitive strategies aim to help you identify the thoughts you want to modify and, at the same time, alter your emotional and behavioral reactions.

Identifying Your Automatic Thoughts

Step one in cognitive work is to open your eyes to your automatic thoughts, which are the rapid, mostly subconscious, mental reactions that happen in response to situations. These thoughts occur so quickly that you may only experience the emotions and not realize the thoughts that triggered them.

Thought Monitoring

Start thinking about times when your anxiety grew. The question to ask yourself could be What thought just went through my mind? The reply, for example, may be pictures, a few words, or even the recall of a particular place or person. Do not immediately judge them as good or bad ones - identify them with wonder. Some of the repetitive anxious thoughts might be:

"Something terrible is going to happen", "I'm not strong enough to cope with this", "No one is very friendly, full of being watchful people", "I'm under threat", "I'm going to become totally out of control", "What a disaster it will be."

The Thought Record

The thought record is a handy tool for recognizing and analyzing one's thought patterns by presenting them in a written and visual form. You need to write down when you find anxiety growing:

The situation (where you were, what happened)

Your feeling and degree (anxiety 7/10)

The only automatic thought(s) that occurred

Information that supports the thought

Information that goes against the thought

The revised version of the thought

The feeling is now associated with the balanced thought

This helps to detach from the initial emotional reactions and view the thoughts in a more neutral light.

Cognitive Restructuring Techniques

First, you should identify and acknowledge any problematic issues in your thoughts. After that, you can start to create more balanced and supportive ways of thinking. This is not about pretending or practicing positive thinking - it is about truthfulness and helpfulness.

Evidence Examination

Once you recognize a worried thought, inquire within:

What facts can prove this idea? Which facts contradict it?

Am I looking at the whole picture?

If a friend had this thought, what advice would I give him?

What's the most probable way of viewing the present case?

This method works to eliminate one of the biases, the confirmation bias, that perpetuates anxious thinking by calling for evidence that contradicts it.

First, estimate the probability/value of the fearful situation (assign it a specific percentage). Next, examine occurrences of similar events (how often does this particular bad thing happen?)

The Worry Window

The inability to constantly eliminate worry often leads to an increased intensity of the concern. The best solution is to represent a unique worry time of only 15 minutes a day. Any such worries that crop up at other times should be reminded that they can only be addressed during the designated worry time. Worry time includes:

Jot down your anxiety issues

Divide the worries according to the categories of solvable and unsolvable ones

Set the step-by-step goals that can lead you to solving the problems for which you are sure of the ways to deal with them

Use relief methods for those tricky situations that you cannot solve

Thought Stopping and Redirection

In the event of recurring concerned thoughts, you:

Tell yourself in a firm voice, Stop!

Do three deep breathing exercises

Shift your focus to the present or an intended activity

Accomplish a task that needs cognitive functions, such as counting backwards from 100 by 7s or listing items of the chosen category

The secret is to have an alternative action or goal ready to start immediately after you stop, rather than trying to clear your mind of thoughts.

Cognitive Defusion Techniques

There are times when the objective is not to modify the thought content but to change the connection between the thoughts and the person having them. Cognitive defusion involves identifying thoughts as separate from oneself and viewing them as an observer rather than a participant.

Thought Labeling

Thoughts can be structured by practicing thought content labeling instead of being completely absorbed in them.

"I'm having a catastrophic thought."

"This is mind reading."

"I'm fortune-telling again."

"My mind is problem-solving."

These utterances frame the experience in a way that is emotionally less engaging; hence, the user's brain may interpret it as less concerning.

The Observer Self

Think of yourself as an observer who watches the thoughts instead of having the same characteristics as them. You may picture:

Wander of thoughts as clouds over the sky of your mind

Your understanding is a stage where various characters express different thoughts

Thinking as fellow travelers on a vehicle you're steering

You are monitoring thoughts as if they were a reel in a cinema

The imagery helps the person grasp that it is not the thoughts themselves, but the presence, which is the cognizance that gives rise to the thoughts, that is the reality.

Mindfulness and Present-Moment Awareness

Most of the time, anxiety is very closely related to the idea of mental time travel -a scenario of future events or a stressful revisiting of the past. Essentially, Mindfulness creates a kind of safe-house experience that keeps the person in the present moment, where anxiety is less powerful.

The STOP Technique

Suppose anxious thoughts appear and you:

Stop what you're doing

Take a deep breath

Check out the thoughts and feelings that you have

Go on, but with a purpose, not a reaction

Conscious control is exercised through a brief inhibition between a stimulus and response, thus permitting more deliberate behavior.

Mindful Thought Observation

Get the practice of recognizing the thoughts that come uninvited without giving in to them:

Discerning the moment when thoughts come up

Looking at these thoughts without labeling or judging

Bringing them along without having a battle or giving any more info

Giving your focus back to the here and now

Such a practice strengthens the mental muscle capable of disengaging from unbidden thoughts that are of no help to you.

Developing Balanced Thinking

One of the aims is to become an overly idealistic, positive person while also generating thoughts that are realistic and helpful. Balanced thinking does not deny that there are some problems, but it recognizes the importance of keeping them in proper perspective and the possibility of a solution.

Both/And Thinking

You can replace either/or points of view with both/and statements:

Instead of "This is terrible," you could say "This is difficult AND I can get through it"

Instead of "I'm a failure," you could say "I made a mistake AND I'm getting better with it"

Instead of "Everyone hates me," you could say "Some people might be critical, AND others like me."

The Wise Friend Perspective

While dealing with anxious thoughts, try to think about what a wise, loving friend would say about that situation. Most of the time, we give others more compassion and a more real view than we do ourselves.

Temporal Perspective

Think about how you will perceive this situation at other times:

How will I feel about this tomorrow?

Will this be important a month from now?

What will I be thinking about this situation after five years?

This method is very effective in putting current worries in a much broader perspective, and so it is not at all overwhelming.

Building Cognitive Flexibility

Patterns of thinking that are very one-dimensional worsen anxiety by not allowing you to be flexible in your approach if the situation changes. Cultivating cognitive flexibility, such as the ability to consider multiple perspectives and ideas, strengthens the ability to step back.

Multiple Perspective Exercise

In any case, that is watering your anxiety; come up with not less than three different ways of understanding it:

What would be the most negative/positive interpretation of the situation?

What would be the most realistic interpretation of the situation? What would be the opinion of someone you admire concerning this situation?

Best-Case, Worst-Case, Most-Likely Scenarios

Don't just be worried about the worst cases, rather look at it from a more balanced perspective:

Describe the very worst outcome

Think of the best possible outcome

Find out what is most likely to happen

Prepare step(s) for dealing with the most probable scenario

Most of the time, this mental drill will uncover that what is going to happen in most cases is far from what the anxiety led you to presume.

Working with Core Beliefs

Anxious thoughts can sometimes be the result of core beliefs about oneself, others, and the world. Commonly, anxiety-connected core beliefs may be the following:

"I'm not good enough."

"The world is a scary place."

"Others will reject me if they get to know the real me."

"I have to be perfect to be acceptable."

Core beliefs often lead to feelings of obligation to follow them, no matter what, and to anger when questioned, even if they are not true. However, as is the case with any other kinds of thoughts, these may also be challenged and changed.

Belief Identification

Please take a moment to examine your automatic thoughts and identify the recurring themes they contain. What underlying beliefs could cause these specific thinking patterns? Core beliefs often give examples of completing sentences, such as:

"I am..."

"Other people are..."

"The world is..."

Historical Analysis

Study the sources of these beliefs:

What firsthand experiences could have taught you this belief?

In which ways could this belief have been protective or adaptive at some point?

Is this belief still accurate and helpful in your present life?

Belief Modification

Rather than focusing on totally removing a core belief, concentrate on creating more balanced alternative ones:

Instead of "I'm inadequate," try saying "I have both good and bad traits like everyone."

Instead of "The world is dangerous," create "The world is a mixture of dangers and safety."

Instead of "I must be perfect," say, "I am still growing, but I'm acceptable as I am."

Integrating Cognitive Strategies

Cognitive efforts become most vigorous when combined with different anxiety management tactics. One such physical method can provide the necessary calm for mental work, while another, a lifestyle change, can reduce the stress that intensifies thoughts.

Daily Practices

Use the cognitive strategies that you have learned as a part of your daily routine:

Morning thought checking (starting the day by noticing thinking patterns)

Midday thought records (examining anxious thoughts that arise during the day)

Evening reflection (reviewing how thought patterns influenced your day)

Crisis Planning

Make use of cognitive aids to overcome extreme anxiety:

Have a list of the most powerful cognitive strategies you use at hand and reachable with ease. Come up with balanced thoughts for your most common anxious predictions. Through practice, make the use of cognitive procedures a habit so that they are readily available when you are stressed.

The Limits of Cognitive Approaches

Although the use of cognitive strategies is effective, they do have certain limitations. Eventually, trying to reason oneself out of every single panic feeling is likely to have the opposite effect, becoming another source of stress. Moreover, anxiety sometimes holds valuable data that must not be gotten rid of through normalization only.

Moreover, the demands of cognitive functioning require considerable mental energy and focus, which are likely not to be available in a situation of severe anxiety. That is why it is essential to have a toolkit that encompasses physical, lifestyle, social, and mental strategies.

Remember that replacing deeply rooted negative thought patterns with positive ones requires a considerable amount of time and patience. As you work on these skills, remember that some days are easier than others, and don't forget to be gentle and kind to yourself.

Building Your Cognitive Toolkit

Try out various cognitive methods until you find the ones that best suit your way of thinking and personal life. What works might differ from case to case, your mood, and the severity of your anxiety.

Get a cognitive coping card on which you will write your most effective strategies. It is an external reminder that can become invaluable when anxiety is so high that it is difficult to remember your skills.

The purpose of thought work is not to eliminate all negative or anxious thoughts; that would not be possible nor healthy. Instead, the goal is to cultivate a more flexible and balanced relationship with your thoughts, allowing you to respond to anxiety with wisdom rather than reactivity.

Thoughts can become the greatest allies to anxiety, or they can become tools to calm down. The awareness and practice of more balanced ways of thinking about situations create an emotional space different from the one you used to have.

Cognitive strategies, when combined with physical ones, bring a holistic approach to anxiety management that reconciles the mind and body components of the anxiety experience.

We will discuss lifestyle foundations in the following chapter that help build overall resilience and lower the risk of anxiety. These long-term strategies provide a stable base from which both physical and cognitive methods can work most effectively.

Anxiety Across the Lifespan

Introduction: The Changing Face of Anxiety

Anxiety is not something that stays constant and suddenly appears in middle age. It is a complex experience that evolves as one progresses through different stages of life, influenced by the specific challenges, abilities, and neurobiological changes that define each phase of human development. The knowledge of anxiety symptoms throughout the life cycle is necessary for parents, teachers, health workers, and even the individuals themselves, as it keeps us aware of everyday developmental concerns, as well as those that are problematic and may require intervention.

Each stage of life, from the fear of the unknown in infancy to the contemplation of life's meaning in old age, comes with its own set of risks and benefits. The manner in which anxiety affects a three-year-old child is totally different from the way a teenager, a middle-aged person suffering from career-related problems, or a senior citizen who is troubled by health issues and the approaching end of life, presents anxiety. These dissimilarities are not merely a consequence of different life situations but also result from significant changes in brain development, cognitive abilities, emotional control skills, and social contexts.

The development process of anxiety disorders will depend on various factors. The factors include genetics, temperament, family dynamics, culture, historical issues, and individual experiences. Some individuals are likely to experience the onset of anxiety at a very young age, and this condition will continue throughout their lifetime. Others may only have anxiety disorders during times of stress or change. Besides, some people may go through anxiety that is not consistent across different life stages but is subject to the unique challenges and opportunities of each period.

Understanding anxiety throughout life also unveils vital points of view about strength and recovery. The same neuroplasticity that previously changed anxiety behavior to the worse now also allows for alteration and betterment. Each life stage comes with different possibilities for evolution and healing, and what at one stage might be regarded as an impossible anxiety problem later on may become easier to handle.

Childhood Anxiety: Early Foundations and Developmental

Childhood is the stage of life most responsible for anxiety problems in the future, as the brain grows very fast, and the basis of the emotional regulation patterns is laid down. These years are crucial for children as they are learning the world, their own characters, and last but not least, the way they will react to anxiety and anger.

Infancy and Toddlerhood: The Origins of Security

The very first signs of the behavior that leads to anxiety can already be noticed in infants during their first months of life. In various stressful situations, such as loud noises, sudden movements, or separation from the caregiver, newborns exhibit the most common and clear signs of distress. These are normal and even necessary reactions for survival, but at the same time, they become the first steps for our anxiety system.

At about 6-8 months, stranger anxiety takes over most infants; that is, they become unhappy when a new person comes near. This event in a child's development epitomizes the ability to differentiate between familiar and new faces. Thus, it is a significant evolutionary adaptation that kept the infants of our ancestors close to protective adults. Similarly, separation anxiety usually appears around 12-18 months when children grow a stronger closeness with their primary caregivers and at the same time become aware that people can leave and may not come back.

The emotional quality of the family relationships that the child has with their caregivers has a significant influence on how the child will react to anxiety. Secure attachment relationships, typically characterized by stable and responsive caregiving, enable children to develop a sense of basic trust and safety in the world. These children learn that when they need help, it is available, and they also develop the ability to manage their emotions through the challenges they face.

On the contrary, for instance, children who are subjected to discontinuous, unresponsive, or scary caregiving situations, in which they want to seek protection and security, may exhibit patterns of insecure attachment that can lead to anxiety. They can become very alert and watchful to detect any signs of danger or separation, or they can emotionally disengage to safeguard themselves against getting their hopes up. Psychological processes that occur during the early years may have an impact on anxiety throughout the whole lifespan; however, they are not fixed and can be changed via later positive experiences.

Preschool Years: Imagination and Fear

The preschool years, approximately from the age of 3 to 5, are a period of dramatic development of their cognitive abilities, language skills, and creativity. These achievements are not only the gateways to new worlds of study and imagination but also to new sources of anxiety.

These children learn to imagine what the world would be like if certain things had not happened yet; thus, they can now worry about a future that may be full of dangers, which can also be their own fantasies.

Among the most common anxieties of this period are fear of monsters, the dark, and animals, which, together with the imaginary creatures, are the ones that frighten the children. Although these fears may seem absurd to adults, they are a regular part of the developmental processes that occur in children. Children are trying to distinguish between make-believe and reality. Since their vibrant imaginations sometimes make the scariest things seem very close and even immediate, they can feel quite scared when this happens.

Preschoolers additionally develop more sophisticated emotional regulation skills, but these capabilities are still quite limited. They may be so caught up in the emotion that it is difficult for them to cool down. Tantrums and breakdowns are manifestations of the children's frustration as they do not master the skills of emotional regulation, which can feel particularly limited for growing ones.

The intensity of separation anxiety is such that it usually peaks during the preschool years and points to the children's growing consciousness of their dependence on the adult world while at the same time experiencing the desire for independence.

Arriving at school or daycare is challenging enough for a child without the added stress of navigating a new environment. The child begins forming new relationships, adapting to new expectations, and coping with separation from familiar caregivers.

Anxiety-type symptoms in children with early signs of anxiety disorders can be such that these kids might appear to be extremely clingy, they might be fearful that family members may get hurt, have difficulty with changes, or have somatic complaints like stomach aches or headaches that seem to be anxiety-related rather than caused by physical illness. Still, it is essential to discern between the two -

developmental phase-based fears and more problematic anxiety patterns.

School-Age Children: Social and Performance Pressure

The elementary school years mark the beginning of numerous challenges as children are no longer at home; they are taken to school and must navigate the complex social lives of society. Initially, school performance becomes a focus, and as a result, children start comparing their own intellectual abilities to those of their peers, not only in school but also in sports, appearance, and social skills.

Children in the school-age group are developing more complex cognitive abilities, such as thinking logically and understanding rules and social expectations. In addition, this cognitive growth ignites a child's imagination to create those worrying scenarios. Children can now foresee many different outcomes, become so engrossed in a failure or embarrassing scenario that it is difficult to disengage themselves from it, and become totally engaged in what-if thinking, which can develop into a nervous habit of excessive worrying.

Social anxiety is the one that is most likely to be noticed or to cause the problem during these years when children become conscious of the judgment of others, i.e., peers and the whole social scene.

They are therefore expected to be worried about things such as being teased, excluded, or humiliated in front of classmates. The dreaded public speaking, group activities, and social interactions that were once considered challenges but manageable may now become significant sources of distress for a child.

Moreover, academic anxiety is becoming one of the prevalent types of anxiety as children are obliged to meet more and more standards of performance, and, at the same time, they start to hold opinions about their strengths.

For instance, some children may develop a tendency towards perfectionism. Thus, they will not only put themselves in a challenging situation of constantly setting unrealistically high standards, but also become highly agitated when these expectations are not met. On the other hand, a few of the kids can become dependent on the help of others when faced with failure, thus stopping their own efforts, convinced they will get nowhere and will give up at the slightest challenge.

Generalized anxiety can be in the form of excessive worry about almost every topic, such as parents' health and safety, natural disasters, world events, or just the coming days. For example, these children may frequently ask for reassurance from adults and struggle to make decisions. They may even have some physical signs of anxiety, such as headaches, stomach problems, and sleep problems.

It is during these years of school that the existence of anxiety disorders is more evident. The requests of academic and social performance not only make the visibility of anxiety symptoms but also their capacity to disturb. However, the anxious children may be quiet and compliant, and as a result, they may achieve high grades; hence, the anxiety is ignored since they do not bring it up.

Family and Environmental Factors in Childhood Anxiety

Anxiety in children has not arisen out of nowhere, but it is primarily attributed to the influence of the family, parenting styles, and the environment. Parents who are full of anxiety may, in a way that is not conscious, depict worried ways of thinking or overprotective behaviors, which will be a kind of reinforcement for children's fears. Stress in a family, economic hardships, divorce, or instability in any other aspect not only makes children's anxiety worse but also makes the stage of anxiety become uncertainty and threat.

Parenting styles that are at either end of the spectrum, overprotective or overly critical, have the power to contribute to the development of anxiety. Overprotective parenting can hinder children's development of the confidence to solve their own problems. Critical or demanding parenting can become a source of chronic stress and a fear of failure in the child.

School environments also play an essential role. Schools that are centered on high-stakes testing, competition, and punishment for mistakes may be a cause that will raise anxiety in children of fragile characters. On the contrary, school environments that promote the growth of positive thinking, emotional learning, and a sense of community belonging can be factors that protect against the development of anxiety.

Trauma exposure, such as abuse, neglect, witnessing violence, or going through natural disasters, can raise the likelihood of anxiety disorders in children to a great extent. Besides, continuous stressors that might not be very severe, like bullying, family conflicts, or medical procedures, can make susceptible children anxious.

Adolescent Anxiety: Identity, Independence, and Intensity

The teenage years are perhaps the most unstable period of human life, during which the physical, cognitive, emotional, and social aspects undergo significant changes. It is maybe not that surprising that anxiety gets stronger in these years, as teenagers have to meet the complicated transition from childhood to maturity. At the same time, they are going through the most difficult and pressing times of their lives.

The Adolescent Brain and Emotional Intensity

During the teenage years, the brain of a teenager undergoes a significant transformation that leads to the complete development of the adult brain, which has several positive effects on the situation of anxiety. The limbic system, comprising the amygdala and other parts that process emotions, matures more quickly and extensively than the prefrontal cortex.

The latter is the decision-making part of the brain, which also oversees logical thinking, impulse control, and emotional balance. This disparity in brain development sparks off a tempest of emotional extremes. Teenagers experience feelings just as strong as those of adults, but have a much poorer reserve to manage these intense feelings effectively. As a result, adolescents are more likely to interpret neutral situations as threatening. In addition to this, they are also more sensitive towards social rejection and take part in risk-taking activities, which might be one of the causes of their anxiety.

The teenage brain is also highly receptive to social cues, which typically involve whether the peer group will accept or reject them. According to brain imaging studies, social exclusion is among those uncomfortable situations that are capable of activating physical pain pathways in teenagers, besides the ones that give the feeling of physical pain. Thus, social anxiety and peer-related stress might have the same intensity as physical pain in that period.

Identity Formation and Existential Anxiety

During adolescence (the teenage years), individuals begin to take their identity seriously and ask themselves questions such as: Who am I? What do I believe in? What kind of person do I want to be? At the same time, this identity development process that is done through

70

questioning is a good thing in the long run and a prerequisite for maturation; it can also be one of the primary sources of anxiety.

The teens might be terrified that they are not normal; perhaps they do not belong to any group, and maybe they are doing everything entirely wrong, from friendships and academic work to their future career. At the same time, they are trying to detach themselves from their families but still need some support and guidance, resulting in an internal conflict between autonomy and security needs.

The adolescent brain is also susceptible to social cues, which typically refer to anything related to whether the peer group will accept or reject them. According to brain imaging studies, social exclusion is among those uncomfortable situations that are capable of activating physical pain pathways in teenagers, besides the ones that give the feeling of physical pain. Thus, social anxiety and peer-related stress might have the same intensity as physical pain in that period.

Social Anxiety and Peer Pressure

Social relationships become the most essential part of life for teenagers, and with this increase in social focus, a teen also becomes more prone to social anxiety. The social world for teens can be challenging and unforgiving, with complex hierarchies, unspoken rules, and the constant risk of being humiliated or rejected.

Many adolescents are socially anxious to a degree that it is far beyond typical shyness. They may avoid social situations, experience a panic episode before a social event, or practice safety behaviors like not making eye contact and staying quiet in group settings to such an extent that they are barely noticeable.

The youth's social playgrounds, like Instagram and Facebook, have brought in various aspects of teenage social anxiety that help cause anxiety at any time of the day or the night, like social comparison, cyberbullying, and the fear of missing out. The dilemma of trying to be equal with others while also being different is a frustrating problem that many teenagers face. They want to be part of the group, but at the same time, they want to be true to themselves; these two goals sometimes conflict with each other.

The fear of being different or standing out among others may cause such conformity pressure that it becomes hard for one to express their individuality and authentically develop their unique identity.

Academic and Performance Anxiety

Academic pressures that lead to anxiety often get heavier in high school when students start seriously considering college admissions. The competition for limited places in top universities has become fiercer over the years, leading many high-achieving students to feel stressed by the continuous cycle of hard work and sleepless nights in their pursuit of perfection.

Performance anxiety could contaminate a person's whole life in many ways: for example, test anxiety can hinder academic performance even when the person has been well prepared; perfectionism can lead to procrastinating or overworking, while generalized worry about grades and achievement can cause incessant worrying. Sometimes, school refusal is a characteristic of students who are so apprehensive about the academic environment that they are unable to attend it physically.

The trend of college-level courses, standardized tests, and college preparatory initiatives has produced the phenomenon that some scholars refer to as "hurried child syndrome", which means that adolescents are tightly scheduled and bombarded with academic and extracurricular demands. This condition of stress, if it becomes chronic, may end up as an anxiety disorder and interrupt the normal, healthy growth of the child.

Body Image and Appearance

Teenagers undergo numerous bodily changes during puberty, and these changes occur at varying rates for different individuals. Typically, teenagers are pretty sensitive about their developing bodies. Actually, the time when puberty comes can affect psychological adjustment a lot, and those who are both early and late developers might be very anxious.

Many of the teenagers develop anxiety about their looks, weight, and body image because we live in a very appearance-focused culture. The use of social media and comparison with peers can exacerbate these worries, which may eventually lead to anxiety about not meeting the beauty standards set by others. Accordingly, the appearance-related anxiety can become a source of eating disorders, social isolation, or the overdoing of such activities as grooming and appearance-checking.

Body image and appearance anxiety is a common adolescent issue that, however, can grow into the so-called body dysmorphic disorder for some teenagers. Those, in this case, become so obsessed with the

72

"flaws" they see in their appearance that they are not recognizable by others. The condition may be devastating and is very likely to be accompanied by other anxiety disorders.

Family Dynamics and Independence Struggles

The adolescent quest for independence often results in conflict with the family as kids seek more freedom, while parents are concerned about safety and setting appropriate limits. These typical developmental struggles may become the main anxieties not only for teenagers but also for their parents.

During this period, family conflict may escalate as teenagers doubt and reject family rules and values, instead, attempting to create their own set of beliefs.

Teens may be anxious about letting down their parents while, at the same time, hating the parental control. Parents, on the other hand, may worry about their teenager's decisions and struggle to step in or let them experience the natural consequences.

It is essential to find the right balance between support and independence at this stage. Teenagers need sufficient autonomy to develop their sense of self and self-esteem, while also requiring ongoing support and guidance as they face new challenges. Those families who have a connection and, at the same time, allow an appropriate level of independence are the ones that seemingly enjoy the best adolescent anxiety and adjustment outcomes.

Risk-Taking and Anxiety Paradox

Quite interestingly, an adolescent is portrayed with not only increased anxiety but also greater risk-taking behavior. This seeming paradox arises from the uneven brain development mentioned earlier, where the emotional brain develops first and the rational one later, leading to more emotionally charged and instant gratification-based decisions rather than those considered through consequences by a careful-minded person.

Some adolescents could perform risk-taking acts to be able to manage their anxiety, like stirring up adrenaline, using drugs to escape from anxiety, and so on. At the same time, some teenagers may become so cautious that they would shun away from activities that are part of the normal developmental stage, such as dating, driving, and social events.

Understanding this paradox is crucial for parents and adults who work with teenagers. Through an anxiety lens, what seems like carefree behavior might actually be a way of handling the root cause of anxiety, whereas what looks like over-cautiousness may at the same time be pointing to anxiety that disrupts normal growth.

Adult Anxiety: Responsibility, Relationships, and Life Transitions
Growing up leads to new anxiety sources and challenges of their own. Adults are typically better equipped with coping skills and emotional regulation abilities; however, kids and adolescents also get overwhelmed by complex responsibilities and life pressures, which, in turn, can cause them to experience anxiety and stress.

Early Adulthood: Establishing Independence and Identity
The transition from adolescence to early adulthood, approximately between 18 and 30 years, is a period of numerous significant life changes that might induce anxiety. Essentially, the young adult is typically preoccupied with making decisions to achieve financial independence, pursuing a college course or career, entering into a romantic relationship, and determining which future path is most suitable for them.

The stage, often referred to as "emerging adulthood," is characterized as a time of instability during which new relationships and various aspects of life are explored. Individuals try different experiences and gradually settle into more permanent adult roles. Although this exploration can certainly be exciting, it is also anxiety-producing for young adults as they have to cope with the uncertainty of their choices and futures.

Career-related anxiety is typical for young adults who are in the early stages of their careers and have to deal with the job hunt, the dynamics in the workplace, and the pressure of creating a professional identity. The stress of competing for a job in a tough market, having student loans, and not being quite sure what the economy will do are a few sources of chronic stress that may lead to anxiety disorders.

Relationship anxiety may be another source of stress for young adults when they are starting to establish romantic relationships and seek friendships. Thus, among the issues they may be considering is finding the "right" person, sustaining relationships, or participating in activities that will have a lasting impact on their lives. The use of social media exacerbates these worries by allowing young adults to see the idealized lives of their peers, both in terms of relationships and the achievements that accompany them.

Middle Adulthood: Peak Responsibilities and Pressures

At the stage of middle adulthood (approximately the ages of 30 to 65), a period of life with the most pressures and pinnacle of responsibilities, adults often feel overwhelmed. They assume different roles simultaneously; for example, they may be pursuing their personal careers and family life, taking care of aging parents, while also managing their own health and aging process.

Work anxieties tend to peak during middle adulthood, as individuals face additional job obligations, increased competition in the work environment, and pressure to advance their careers. The "sandwiched generation" dilemma of adults who have the responsibility of caring for both children and their elderly parents is a source of both stress and anxiety, resulting from being overburdened with multiple demands that need handling at one time.

Financial anxiety is complicated more during middle adulthood as people are concerned with saving for retirement, paying for children's education, home loans, and dealing with unexpected financial issues such as medical bills or losing a job. The economic side of these responsibilities, being long-term, can turn into constant anxiety and worry about overplanning.

Parenting anxiety is a source of concern for middle-aged adults who think about their children's safety, growth, and success in the future. The present parenting culture, which highly depends on the concept of perfection and achievement, can lead to the parents having to make the most of the situation and also experiencing this anxiety.

Besides, marriage and relationship anxiety can lead to middle-aged couples who are experiencing the stresses of parenting, financial pressure, and life changes. The peak divorce rate is at this point, and so adults are worrying about relationship satisfaction and stability.

Health Anxiety and Aging Concerns

Adults eventually go through the stages in their 30s, 40s, and 50s when they notice signs of physical aging, and thus, they are most likely to experience health-related anxiety. Thorough medical check-ups can also indicate the development of health problems, and adults may become increasingly aware that they are not immortal and could be vulnerable.

Once health anxiety takes over someone, they cannot stop focusing on their symptoms; they will be looking for doctors all the time, but at the same time, they might be avoiding getting checked because they are scared that they will get bad news.

Health information is more accessible these days than ever through the internet. Still, at the same time, it has created the phenomenon of "cyberchondria," where individuals who search for medical symptoms online conclude that they have serious diseases.

Some adults are so anxious about their physical appearance and the process of aging that they may even suffer from depression, especially in a culture where youth and attractiveness mean everything. This can raise such matters as anxiety about dating, career, or social acceptance in the future.

Career and Professional Development Anxiety

The work situation can be an important source of stress for adults, for example, if they are experiencing job insecurity, conflicts with colleagues, job stagnation, or pressure to advance. The present-day economy's stress on flexibility and continuous learning implies that adults need to develop a new skill set, which can be daunting.

Imposter syndrome

It is widespread among successful adults who constantly think they are not good enough for their roles and fear that others will discover their fakeness. It can result in long-lasting anxiety about the person's performance and a terror of failure. Experts get worried about career changes, transformations, or moves, whether they decide on them by themselves or with others. This is because adults face significant uncertainty about their careers and might even need to learn new skills or work in different industries.

Financial Stress and Security Concerns

Adults worry about money across all income levels, although different types of worries may show up depending on the situation. For example, low-income adults may worry about meeting their basic needs and managing uncontrollable financial conditions, while affluent adults may fear losing their lifestyle and not saving adequately for retirement.

The intricate nature of modern financial planning can generate concerns about the correct execution of investments, the selection of a suitable insurance policy, and the efficient building of a financial safety net.

These anxieties may become more severe because of economic uncertainty and market instability.

Parents nearing retirement are likely to be anxious about whether they have saved enough and how they will manage with a fixed income. The transition from earning to spending savings is a major psychological transition that can instantly ignite a lot of anxiety.

Later Life Anxiety: Wisdom, Vulnerability, and Legacy

Opposite to the belief that worries fade with age, older adults are the ones who encounter anxiety in the face of health decline, social losses, financial security issues, and facing death issues in their later years. While the old might have acquired better coping and emotional regulation skills throughout their lives, they still encounter situations that stress them, over which they have no control.

Physical Health and Medical Anxiety

The natural intensity of health concerns is progressively aging, and old people are more likely to get chronic diseases, lose their mobility, and eventually have their cognition lowered. The medical anxiety may be the apprehension towards diagnosis and treatment, the fear of pain or weakness, or the concern of being a burden on the family because of needing extensive care.

The healthcare system is a significant source of anxiety for the elderly who are going through the process of finding their way through the complicated medical system, dealing with a lot of healthcare providers, and having to make the tough decision of the best course of treatment. The fear of medical procedures, the side effects, and the uncertainty of the prognosis are the reasons why anxiety can be very high.

Cognitive changes, which are even normal for the person's age and concern memory and processing speed, can be a cause of exaggerated fears of developing dementia or Alzheimer's disease. Older adults may monitor their memory with extreme care to the point where they become obsessed with that and cognitive decline anxiety.

Social Isolation and Loneliness

Social anxiety of elderly people is mainly connected to their aging process, through which they become more and more socially isolated because friends and family members either die, move away, or are less available due to their own health issues. One can lose important social contacts established at work due to retirement, and mobility limitations can make it difficult to keep up with social activities.

The disappearance of social roles, which had been the primary source of identity and life purpose during adulthood, can cause existential anxiety about the meaning and relevance of life. Older adults may be concerned about being forgotten or becoming obsolete in a rapidly changing world.

Technology anxiety is a growing problem among older adults, who feel abandoned by rapid technological changes and worry about their ability to communicate with younger family members or use online services, increasingly replacing traditional business methods.

Financial Security in Retirement

Financial insecurity, a source of anxiety throughout life, is a major concern in later years. Older people are living on fixed incomes, healthcare is becoming more expensive, and they are uncertain how long their savings will last. The complicated nature of Medicare, Social Security, and retirement planning can induce a fear of making a wrong decision, which in turn could lead to financial insecurity.

Some seniors develop anxiety about the possibility of being utterly dependent on their grown-up kids or having to undergo costly long-term care, which will rapidly exhaust their savings. The healthcare cost, together with prescription medications, is a source of anxiety that can easily become a nightmare for those living on a limited budget.

Mortality, Anxiety, and Legacy Concerns

Coming to terms with death is more direct in the senior years as elders have to deal with the deaths of their acquaintances and their own deteriorating health. Death anxiety can involve terror of the dying process, fear of the unknown, or the dreadful thought of separation from those whom we care for.

Legacy angst refers

to the fear of death and time after death. For older people, it is also about how meaningful life has been and the extent of one's impact on the world. Some of these older people may worry about their relationships with family, feel guilty about past lives, and even want to be remembered through the things they have taught younger generations.

Some seniors become so worried to the point of anxiety that they imagine themselves as a burden to their families when they get old, and that it is going to be a sad and complex process for the loved ones who will have to make arrangements for their care and attend to their needs. The issues concerning family, assistance, and caregiving create immense emotional distress for the individual.

Adapting to Physical and Cognitive Changes

Normal aging is associated with a slow but sure decline in physical abilities, sensory functions, and cognitive processing, which, unfortunately, might cause anxiety even if any serious health problems do not accompany them. At the same time, changes in vision and hearing can make older adults feel vulnerable, and if social isolation is added to that, it will be even worse. Loss of balance and immobility may definitely contribute to the feeling of anxiety about having a fall and hurting oneself.

Sleep changes are typical in older adults and could be the reason for anxiety, both as a symptom and as a source. The anxiety surrounding sleep difficulties can cause a cycle in which the sleeplessness and anxiety reinforce each other.

Driving anxiety is one of the significant problems of older adults who are constantly worried about whether they will be able to drive safely, and at the same time, feel anxious about losing their independence if they stop moving. The decision to give up driving is the hardest and makes one the most nervous.

Positive Aspects of Aging and Resilience

On the one hand, there is a long list of difficult situations; on the other hand, a lot of older adults make it to the list of the most resilient people and may have less anxiety than younger adults. The lens of life experience provides the perspective and hedges that help an older person separate serious problems from mere inconveniences.

Older adults frequently acknowledge greater proficiency in emotional regulation and concentration on positive experiences while letting go of minor annoyances. The emotional selectivity, in this case, is a form of immunization against the anxiety that affects the individual to a certain extent.

With the support of life experience, more realistic expectations, and better coping strategies, older adults become wiser. Many older adults report feeling more confident about their personality and not so much concerned about the opinions of others, a factor that can contribute to the lowering of social anxiety.

Usually, people move forward spiritually with age, and this can be a great source of comfort and a way of life that helps to face existential anxiety. Most of the elderly reveal that they are now more connected to something greater than themselves, whether it be a religious faith, nature, or a concern for people in need.

Generational and Cultural Influences

Fear is not totally separated from the culture, and every parent generation has to tackle its own specific historical circumstances that, on an emotional level, shape fear and anxiety. Identifying these generational and cultural influences proves to be a helpful tool in understanding why anxiety can unfold differently in different generational and cultural groups.

Historical Context and Generational Anxiety

Every generation finds itself living through certain historical events that challenge its perspective on life and become a source of anxiety that it experiences. The Silent Generation (born 1928-1945) experienced the Great Depression and World War II, events that might have shaped their views on security, authority, and future planning.

The social changes of the 1960s and 1970s, including the civil rights movements, the Vietnam War, and shifting social norms, were the issues that the Baby Boomers (born 1946-1964) had to contend with. Their patterns of concern may be linked to social changes and exhibit signs of rebelling against the politically established groups that comprise the power structures.

Generation X (born 1965-1980) was a community that lived through an economic recession, experienced increasing divorce rates, and saw the idea of a dual-career family gaining traction. Work-life issues, financial stability, and relationship issues might be the anxiety-related topics that they would bring up if talking about their childhood experiences.

Millennials (born 1981-1996) have been surrounded by economic uncertainty, student loan debt, interruptions of traditional life paths, and the rise of social media. Their anxiety problems may come from insecure jobs, money worries, and comparison to others via social media.

Generation Z (born 1997-2012) has been witnessing the world with climate change anxieties, school shootings, political tension, and non-stop digital connectivity since their childhood. Their worry might be a mix of existential threats, safety concerns, and an overload of information.

Cultural and Ethnic Considerations

Different cultures vary in their perspectives on mental health, emotional expression, family roles, and help-seeking behaviors.

Some cultures may view anxiety as selfish and inappropriate, yet they emphasize collective well-being, a common trait of cultures that prioritize the individual. Thus, anxiety about personal issues might be perceived as either appropriate or not. On the other hand, some cultures may be so stigmatizing of mental health problems that it becomes a great challenge for people to get help or even recognize their anxiety.

Different cultural expressions of anxiety may differ a lot. For example, Western cultures typically concentrate on psychological symptoms, whereas other cultures might consider physical symptoms to be most important or that spiritual factors cause anxiety. Liking these cultural differences is a vital step towards giving proper help and care.

Immigration and acculturation may be two of the main reasons for the creation of anxiety patterns, as the persons involved have to deal with the different cultural expectations and values. Second-generation immigrants may be anxious about the culture of their ancestors versus the mainstream culture.

Socioeconomic Factors

Socioeconomic status is one of the main factors that shape anxiety behavior over the course of a person's life. Those from impoverished families with low income and level of education may be overwhelmed by constant stressful situations caused by living in unsafe neighborhoods, being financially insecure, and having less access to resources. All these issues can eventually lead to the development of anxiety disorders.

In any case, all people in society are exposed to anxiety problems. However, the manifestation of anxiety in different levels of socioeconomic status may vary. For example, in the sphere of high socioeconomic status, the situation may be such that there will be more resources for anxiety management. Still, at the same time, there will be more pressure put on a person to keep their status and to succeed in that bigger way, which eventually will lead to performance anxiety.

The possibility of getting professional medical help for the psychological condition varies a lot depending on the socioeconomic status of a family. In particular, people with low incomes often have minimal access to treatment options. The difference in access to care can lead to different patterns of anxiety development and persistence throughout the lifespan.

Developmental Interventions and Support

Identifying anxiety across various life stages is the first step towards implementing prevention, intervention, and support methods that are equally suited to each stage of development. The process that will be effective in treating a child's anxieties may not be suitable for a teenager or an older adult.

Early Intervention and Prevention

The better the long-term outcomes of anxiety problems, the sooner the identification and the ways of treatment are carried out. This does not primarily entail formal treatment, only providing support and teaching coping skills that can halt/reverse the development of anxiety patterns.

Younger children are mostly treated through parental education and family support programs. Parents can learn skills to respond to an anxious child in a way that builds confidence, rather than through avoidance. This approach not only motivates the child to face their fears but also helps them acquire other anxiety-coping skills.

The school-based prevention programs that introduce emotional regulation skills, stress management, and the quality of resilience can definitely help kids and teenagers have new mechanisms to tackle anxiety, which is not yet problematic.

Developmental Considerations in Treatment

The treatments that accompany different methods must be tailored to the individual's stage of development and ability. We can imagine that young children will benefit from therapy through play and family-based activities, whereas adolescents will be more inclined to group therapy and peer support approaches.

The methods of treatment for adults are more cognitive-focused, with logical reasoning as the primary tool; thus, mature reasoning skills are heavily used in adult treatment, whereas, in treatments for senior citizens, we find a need to take into account issues of physical health as well as make changes so that they are compatible with the sensory or cognitive disabilities of older adults.

The timing of interventions can be the key element. The developmental transitions can often turn out to be great opportunities for change, as individuals are already adjusting to new situations and may therefore be more receptive to learning new ways of coping.

Building Resilience Across the Lifespan

It is way better to prevent or treat anxiety issues before they develop rather than simply treating them. There is a growing consensus on the importance of building resilience and developing coping skills throughout the various stages of development. Teaching individuals to manage stress, control their emotions, stay connected socially, and adapt to life's changes is part of it.

Building resilience is a different condition at different stages in life. Still, it primarily involves developing a sense of competence and self-efficacy, maintaining supportive relationships, discovering meaning and purpose, and practicing self-care and stress management.

Lifestyle Foundations That Anchor You

The Power of Daily Rhythms

Even though breathing exercises and cognitive techniques can very quickly calm anxiety, changes that last long will need your attention on the lifestyle factors that are either helping or harming your mental health. Think of these factors as being the earth in which your mental health grows—when the world is full of nutrients and properly tended, you are naturally more resistant to the occurrence of the stressful situations of life.

Most people concentrate only on the management of anxiety symptoms, and they ignore the lifestyle foundations that cause the symptoms. It is like trying to fill a broken bucket with water—you can add water all the time, but if you do not mend the holes, the bucket will not hold the water effectively.

Six lifestyle factors that have the most influence on anxiety are sleep, nutrition, exercise, stress management, social connections, and environmental influences. The six components are interconnected in a way that poor sleep affects nutrition, which in turn affects the energy for exercise. This, in turn, affects your stress level, which affects your social relationships, thus creating a chain of effects that either helps or hinders your anxiety management.

Sleep: The Foundation of Emotional Regulation

Of all the lifestyle factors, sleep ranks number one in anxiety management. Basically, when you do not get enough sleep, the part of the brain responsible for detecting dangers goes into overdrive, while the abilities of emotional regulation become weaker. This development is like a perfect storm that leads to high anxiety levels.

The Sleep-Anxiety Link

In the course of sleep, your brain sorts out, stores, and gets rid of all the waste products after the day's metabolic processes. Sleep deprivation interrupts these functions and causes changes in anxiety symptoms:

The amygdala hijacks your brain, becoming overreactive to potential threats. At the same time, the prefrontal cortex, which is responsible for logic, emotional regulation, and other cognitive functions, becomes less active. Therefore, you have a high probability of overestimating danger and lacking control of your feelings.

Stress hormone levels also rise due to sleep deprivation. Inadequate sleep will be followed by high cortisone levels, which will cause a state of constant stress resulting in anxiety susceptibility. Moreover, the lack of sleep affects the production of neurotransmitters such as serotonin and GABA, which are essential for regulating mood and inducing calmness.

Sleep Hygiene On-Point

Behaviors that lead to fewer interrupted sleeping hours include even minor changes in the person's habits, as well as environmental modifications that improve their situation.

Timing and Consistency: The circadian clock within your body functions that way when it is given a specific time for sleep and the same time for waking up, every day without exception (even weekends). The internal self-regulation of the body clock will thus be normalized, making it easier for people to both fall asleep and wake up.

Pre-Sleep Ritual: Create a calming ritual that signals to your body it is time to relax. Dimming the lights, taking a warm bath, reading, gentle stretching, or using relaxation methods would all be good ways to start the ritual. Practicing this routine 30-60 minutes before your intended sleep time will yield the desired effects.

Sleep Environment: The bedroom should be calm (between 65-68°F), dark, and quiet. If needed, use blackout curtains, eye masks, or a white noise machine. Your mattress and pillows should be both comfortable and supportive. The bedroom should be a place for sleeping and sex only—working out, watching television, or doing other activities that get you stimulated is not recommended.

Light Exposure: Light plays a crucial role in regulating the sleep-wake cycle. Bright light in the morning and during the day, especially natural sunlight, should be your primary source of light exposure. Turn off the lights and refrain from using screens for at least one hour before going to sleep. If you must use devices, consider using blue light-blocking glasses and apps that filter out blue light.

Handling Sleep Anxiety

Those who suffer from anxiety and worry quite often develop anxiety concerning sleep as well, thus worrying whether they will be able to get to sleep and stay asleep. Hence, a paradox arises in which trying to sleep actually prevents one from falling asleep.

If you find that your thoughts are preventing you from falling asleep, try the "20-minute rule": if you are unable to fall asleep within 20 minutes of lying down, get up and engage in a quiet, non-stimulating activity until you feel sleepy. This is a way to ensure that your bed is not a place you associate with wakefulness and worry.

Do not make a fuss about being wide awake and instead, practice the art of acceptance. Remind yourself that rest is still beneficial, even when you are not asleep, and that your body will rest at the right time. Most of the time, the pressure to sleep is the cause of the very arousal that keeps one awake.

Napping Guidelines

Naps can be reenergizing, but they can also disturb nighttime sleep if not properly timed. If you feel the need to take a nap, keep it brief (20-30 minutes) and avoid napping after 3 PM. A nap of longer duration or one taken late in the day can make it difficult for you to fall asleep at your bedtime.

Nutrition: Fueling Calm or Anxiety

Your diet impacts the brain chemicals, blood sugar stability, and the general energy levels of the body, all of which are the main reasons for the development of anxiety. There is no one "anti-anxiety diet," but with the help of the nutrition principles, emotional stability can still be maintained.

Blood Sugar and Anxiety

Rapid changes in blood sugar can mimic and provoke the symptoms of anxiety. The situation when blood sugar falls rapidly makes the body release stress hormones to provide the needed glucose from the storage, thus bringing physical symptoms identical to anxiety: trembling, fast heartbeat, inability to focus, and irritability.

Keeping blood sugar at a healthy level requires:

Eating small meals and snacks at regular intervals instead of going without food for a long time

Adding protein and good fats to carbohydrates so that the absorption of the carbohydrates will be slower

Selecting low-sugar, high-complex-carbohydrate foods if there is an option

Knowing how each food item affects your blood sugar level response

Caffeine Considerations

Caffeine is a stimulant that, if put in an already delicate situation, might worsen the anxiety symptoms. The caffeine will elevate your heart rate, might make you feel nervous, and might also affect the quality of your sleep. On the other hand, caffeine has different effects on different people – some individuals can consume moderate amounts without any discomfort, while others are more susceptible to its effects.

If you consume caffeine, it is essential to be aware of how your body reacts to it. Analyze the relationship between your anxiety levels and high- and low-caffeine days.

If you choose to cut down on your caffeine intake, make sure the process is gradual so that you do not get withdrawal symptoms such as headaches and fatigue, which may lead to a temporary rise in anxiety.

Alcohol and Anxiety

The reason why people often choose to drink alcohol to deal with anxiety is that it gives a speedy, relaxing effect. On the other hand, alcohol has the potential to make anxiety worse in multiple ways:

Alcohol changes the quality of sleep, especially the REM sleep, which results in anxiety the next day. As alcohol is being metabolized, there is also the chance of creating rebound anxiety. With regular use, there is the risk of tolerance and dependence that, in turn, raises baseline anxiety levels.

If you are a drinker, be sure that you are not deceiving yourself and that alcohol is not a contributor to the development of your anxiety puzzle, rather than being a real solution. Try to limit your consumption and check how you feel on days when you have drunk versus days when you have abstained.

Nutrients for Nervous System Support

Though dietary supplements are not miraculous healers, it will be much healthier to take some nutrient-rich foods into the diet for the purpose of supporting the nervous system:

Omega-3 fatty acids, derived from fish, walnuts, and flaxseeds, support brain health and may potentially alleviate anxiety triggered by the body's inflammatory response. Magnesium is responsible for the process of muscles relaxing and the workings of the nervous system - quite a few people get very little magnesium from their diets.

B vitamins, mainly B6 and B12, carry out the functions essential for the production of neurotransmitters.

Probiotics are turning out to be significant in the gut-brain axis. A well-functioning gut microbiome may determine a person's mood and anxiety level, although this field is still under research.

Always consult a healthcare professional before taking any supplements to avoid drug interactions and ensure proper dosing.

Exercise: Moving Toward Calm

One of the leading causes of anxiety can be well controlled through regular physical exercise, which is indeed one of the most effective interventions. Exercising gives the person both immediate anxiety relief and a long-term capacity for stress resistance. These effects occur through various means, including lowering stress hormone levels, increasing endorphin levels, improving sleep quality, boosting self-worth, and releasing nervous energy in a controlled manner.

The Immediate Effects

Once a person has exercised, a single session can reduce anxiety levels for several hours after the activity is completed. The reason is that exercise eliminates stress hormones (for example, cortisol and adrenaline) and, at the same time, encourages the secretion of endorphins and other mood-lifting chemicals.

The stress response cycle can also be positively sidestepped through exercise. Your body prepares for fighting or running away, but you do not actually fight or escape, so the energy that causes arousal remains within your system. You can release this energy through physical activity.

Long-Term Benefits

One of the regular exercises that can be done is changing the person's vulnerability to anxiety in a positive way.

Improved cardiovascular health makes one less reactive to stress

Better sleep quality reduces anxiety susceptibility

Increased confidence in your physical capabilities generalizes to other areas

Regular engagement in exercise goals builds self-efficacy

Time spent outdoors thus provides more than enough mental health benefits

Finding Your Exercise Approach

An exercise program that will work out for you is the one you are most likely to follow. Think about:

- Your current fitness level and any physical limitations
- Time constraints and schedule preferences
- Whether you prefer solo or group activities
- Indoor versus outdoor preferences
- High-intensity versus gentle movement preferences

Exercise for Different Anxiety Types

Different anxiety symptoms can be managed at times through various exercise routines. For high-energy anxiety accompanied by restlessness, engaging in vigorous activities can help discharge excess energy.

For anxiety with muscle tension, yoga or stretching can promote both physical and mental relaxation. For anxiety with low energy or depression, gentle activities like walking or swimming can improve mood without overwhelming your system.

When we discuss social anxiety, a person may feel more comfortable engaging in activities alone initially; however, group fitness classes can be an excellent option for gaining positive social exposure in a safe and organized setting.

Your First Exercise Routine

If you are not already active, it is advisable that you start small and then gradually build up. Even 10-15 minutes of daily movement can provide numerous benefits.

Consider:

Going for walks during your lunch breaks or while you are on the phone

Choosing to use the stairs rather than the elevators

Leaving your car at a spot that is a bit far from your destination

Using bodyweight exercises during TV commercials

Dancing to music while doing household chores

The main thing is consistency rather than the level of intensity. Maintaining a moderate routine is more beneficial than following a very intense program that you stop after two weeks.

Stress Management: Building Your Buffer Zone

Although it is not possible to eliminate all stress from your life, you can certainly develop more effective ways to manage it. Proper stress management is a good way to stop the buildup of chronic stress that leads to an increase in anxiety vulnerability.

Identifying Your Stress Patterns

It's just like you traced your anxiety triggers; you also need to figure out your stress pattern:

Which situations always stress you out?

How do you usually react to stress?

What are the first signs of stress getting out of control that you have?

Which stress management methods that you have tried in the past were successful?

Time Management and Boundaries

Poor time management and lack of firm boundaries are typical causes of chronic stress. Imagine:

Prioritization: Learn to distinguish between what is urgent and what is essential to do. Many people focus their efforts on urgent but unimportant tasks, while simultaneously overlooking important but non-urgent ones.

Saying No: A yes to one thing is simultaneously a no to something else. Get into the habit of saying no to more commitments that are not in line with your priorities or will use up your energy.

Realistic Planning: Rather than relying on punctual time planning, ensure that you build your schedules with buffer times. It not only reduces the stress of being late but also gives you a chance to enjoy the unexpected delays.

Delegation: Find the tasks that others could do, so that you will be able to concentrate on the tasks that only you can do.

Regular Stress Release

Come up with regular methods of releasing pent-up stress:

Daily relaxation techniques (breathing exercises, meditation, progressive muscle relaxation)

Weekly stress-releasing activities (massage, hobbies, social time)

Monthly or seasonal bigger releases (vacations, retreats, major fun activities)

Problem-Solving vs. Acceptance

There are only a few stressors that can be solved through action, while most of them demand acceptance. Cultivate the necessary abilities for both cases:

If the problem is resolvable, handle it by means of a structured problem-solving approach: set the problem in the proper perspective, come up with several possible solutions, assess each of them, choose the best one to be put into action, and lastly evaluate the results.

In situations that cannot be changed, try to focus on acceptance strategies: recognizing reality without necessarily agreeing with it, concentrating on aspects that are under your control, discovering the reasons to live or the growth opportunities, and gradually practicing letting go.

Social Connections: The Anxiety Antidote

Social beings are humans in normal circumstances, and our relations significantly reflect on our psychological health. Strong social connections provide not only emotional support but also practical assistance, different perspectives, and a sense of belonging to a group that offers protection against anxiety.

Quality Over Quantity

The impact of relationships is not mostly about the number you have, but about their quality instead. In fact, the quality of a few deep, supportive relationships is more beneficial than the quantity of many superficial ones. Good quality relationships are those that are based on mutual trust and respect, provide emotional support in difficult situations, allow you to be your true self, feature both parties giving and taking equally, and have common interests or values.

Building Social Support

If the extent of your social support network is not satisfactory, it is highly recommended that you develop existing relationships by sharing more authentically. Participating in groups that match your interests, values, or life circumstances. Volunteering for the causes that matter to you the most. Take a class or do an activity in which you will find people with the same interests and mindset. Act in the manner that reflects the type of friend you would like to have.

Managing Social Anxiety in Relationships

If social anxiety is the main reason for isolation:

Go for low-pressure social events first

Be kind to yourself, even when social interactions were not great

Think that everyone is most likely concerned with themselves and not in judging you

Question your ideas when estimating what others are thinking

Increase your comfort zone slowly instead of escaping from all social encounters

Digital Connection Considerations

Social media and digital communication can provide easier access to real-world relationships; nevertheless, they ought not to replace face-to-face interaction completely. Take notice of the way digital connections affect your mood and anxiety levels. Some may find that social media causes their anxiety to escalate through comparison or to be overwhelmed with information.

Environmental Influences

Your physical environment has a significant impact on your emotional state. Making places that are tranquil and that allow anxiety to fade can bring lasting benefits.

Home Environment

Your place of residence should be a refuge where you can relax and energize yourself:

Remove the unnecessary things from the rooms to avoid visual overwhelm

Put in nature the likes of pure and bright sun

Make the areas where the activities happen mainly for relaxation

Big brown and more light are what people like most

Do your best to lessen the sound pollution in the area

Attempt to keep the spots decently clean and neat

Work Environment

If it is possible, adapt your workplace to be more anxiety-friendly:

Decorate your area with things that matter to you

Make sure you have enough light and a comfortable chair

If it is allowed to use flowers or other natural things

Do not mix work with your personal area

Do not work all the time and get some fresh air or go for a walk

Technology Boundaries

Even though technology is good and comes with many benefits, it can also be the cause of anxiety through too much information, comparing with others, and being constantly connected.

Try having some times or places where you do not use your phone. Do not watch the news if it makes you more anxious. Only follow people who bring you good in social media. Use tech only during the time you decided not to be compulsive. Sometimes, turn off your devices before going to sleep so that you can rest better.

Creating Your Personal Lifestyle Plan

Do not rush into changes in your lifestyle, and avoid trying to improve everything at once. You can work on your lifestyle factor one by one and see which lifestyle factor would have the most significant impact on your anxiety if improved.

The 1% Better Approach

Repeated small and consistent acts of improvement add up to great results with time. Rather than turning your life upside down in an unsustainable manner, aim to be 1% better every day in any area you choose. This could be:

By going to bed 15 minutes earlier every night until you get your desired bedtime

Increasing the number of vegetables that you eat by one serving

Adding 5 minutes to your daily walk each day

Practicing one minute of deep breathing every day

Tracking and Adjusting

Make a simple note of your lifestyle factors and how your anxiety levels vary with them. This allows you to recognize the changes that bring the most relief, thereby maintaining your motivation to improve.

Self-Compassion in Change

Lifestyle changes are gradual, and setbacks occur. If you find that you are not quite up to your own expectations, then treat yourself nicely. Progress is not a straight line, and the tendency to become perfect in lifestyle changes is just another source of anxiety. Remember, these lifestyle changes are the main pillars that support one another; often, one area of change is almost naturally endorsed by others. A good night's sleep will not only make you feel like you've eaten healthily; it will also improve your overall well-being. Still, it will also provide the energy you need for exercise, reduce stress associated with exercise, and thus lead to better relationships and an upward spiral of well-being.

One of the main points is not perfection, but instead creating a lifestyle that supports your mental health and provides a sense of stability when navigating life's challenging times. Whenever your needs for sleep, nutrition, movement, stress management, connection, and environmental support are fulfilled, you become resilient, and anxiety can be less of a problem for you when it occurs.

Cultivating Emotional Resilience

The Inner Strength That Sustains You

Emotional resilience can be seen as the psychological equivalent of "get-up-and-go". It's your ability to handle emotional challenges, bounce back from defeat, and remain emotionally stable in the face of life's regular ups and downs. Whereas breathing techniques provide instant relief and lifestyle changes offer foundational support, emotional resilience embodies a profound shift in one's relationship with the occurrence of the most dreadful experiences, even anxiety.

Images depict two individuals: one has developed enhanced coping skills, while the other has not. Both figures are the same and face the same stressful situation: losing their jobs. Person A is devastated by negative thoughts, becomes emotionally numb within, and is still in misery after several months of the tragedy. Conversely, Person B feels the shock and disappointment but soon switches to problem-solving mode, keeps faith even in the dark tunnel of the future, and transforms the difficulty into a source of growth and change. The variation is not due to their conditions or even their initial emotional reactions, but it lies in their emotional resilience.

The development of emotional resilience does not involve shutting down emotions or denying the existence of unpleasant feelings. On the contrary, it is about experiencing all the emotions that comprise the human condition while maintaining one's psychological stability and effectiveness at work. Such as anxiety, sadness, anger, and fear, resilient individuals feel their emotions, but they are not masters of them.

It is possible to develop this ability at any time in one's life. It appears that some individuals are born with greater resilience due to their genetic makeup, early experiences, or temperament; however, the main components of emotional resilience can be learned and developed through purposeful practice. This procedure involves acquiring specific skills, attitudes, and habits that form the foundation of one's emotional stability and can serve as the person's adaptive response to a given difficulty.

Understanding Emotional Resilience

Emotional resilience is a complex system composed of several interconnected levels. Emotional awareness, the ability to observe and assess one's emotional condition as and when it happens,

is the very lowest level. Many people are emotionally on autopilot, and during emotional upheavals, they do not consciously recognize their feelings. Hence, their skillful reaction will be minimal due to a lack of awareness.

On the second level, emotional regulation involves the ability to influence the intensity, duration, and expression of your feelings. It is not only that emotions are suppressed or tightly controlled, but the person is gaining more power over them. The process of emotional regulation consists of the following skills: self-soothing during periods of distress, maintaining one's perspective or frame of reference throughout strong emotions, and deciding to respond helpfully instead of giving in to anger or frustration.

The third level encompasses all the positives that a person can see in a situation. It includes the ability to see and accept different opinions on the same thing, i.e., being flexible cognitively. An optimistic interpretation of a situation, allowing a person to grow and learn from it rather than falling into despair and remaining stagnant, is the cognitive aspect of resiliency. The ability to discover new aspects of life and find explanations in challenging life situations is a characteristic of resilient people. They are also capable of seeing setbacks as temporary rather than permanent and of maintaining a positive outlook, even in the darkest hours of life.

Behavioral flexibility is an aspect of resilience, defined as the ability to adjust your actions and plans in response to new situations. Instead of sticking with the same strategies regardless of the problem, resilient individuals can change their reactions to meet the requirements of different circumstances.

Developing emotional resilience begins with cultivating a nuanced understanding of one's emotional landscape. Most people possess a fundamental emotional vocabulary and usually refer to their feelings with words like "good", "bad", "fine", or "stressed". This emotional incapacity to read limits the ability to react adequately in various emotional situations.

To begin with, you should learn to distinguish between various emotional states with greater accuracy. Instead of just feeling "bad", you could be feeling disappointment, frustration, loneliness, overwhelm, or regret. Each of these emotions has its own unique content and may require different responses.

One way to build an emotional vocabulary list is to gather words that depict different emotional states. Look for the slight differences in similar emotions-the line between anxiety and excitement, between sadness and grief, and so on. These differences are significant because they enable a correct response.

During the day, you may engage in emotional check-in activities. It may involve setting a few reminders during which one is supposed to stop and ask themselves: "What is my feeling right now?" Attempt to identify not only the primary emotion but also any other feelings in the background that may be present. In this case, you may find that you are mostly excited about a forthcoming event, but also experience some anxiety about your performance.

Body-Based Emotional Awareness

Feeling emotions is a process of embodiment, and by recognizing how various feelings manifest in your body, you will be able to identify them even at an early stage. Keep in touch with the bodily changes that happen during emotional shifts.

Worry may be felt as a tightness in the chest, a full stomach, or stiff muscles. Anger can be identified by symptoms such as jaw clenching, tightness in the shoulders, or a rise in body temperature. Grief may be likened to a feeling of heaviness in the chest or a general sense of fatigue throughout the body. Happiness may be identified with the sense of lightness, vigor, or expansion of the chest.

Such body-centered consciousness acts as a preliminary medical kit, notifying you of the alternative of the same sort, but before they get too strong. When you feel your shoulders are tense or your breathing is shallow, you can connect with your inner self to identify the emotion present.

Emotional Patterns and Triggers

Just like analyzing your anxiety triggers and patterns, understanding the general emotional patterns that are possible gives you a bigger emotional battery. Find out the situations that most likely evoke emotional responses, how different feelings progress, and last but not least, what your usual way of getting out of the sad times is.

Some people feel that their emotions change rapidly, whereas others claim to experience prolonged emotional states. Some people observe that one emotion leads to another - for example, anxiety may turn into irritation, or sadness may be accompanied by self-reproach. Knowing these personal patterns helps you to foresee and prepare for emotional hardships.

Emotional Regulation Strategies

Emotional regulation is the process of developing the skills necessary to manage emotions effectively when they arise. The goal is not to eliminate difficult emotions, as they often provide essential information and encourage the required actions, but to mitigate their intensity so that they do not overwhelm you or lead to unhelpful behaviors.

The RAIN Technique

RAIN is a mnemonic that outlines a step-by-step method for dealing with intense emotions. The letters refer to Recognition, Allowing, Investigation, and Non-identification (or Nurturing).

Recognition of an emotion involves identifying it and distinguishing it from your thoughts and judgments. In terms of sound, it is similar to: "I feel nervous and therefore I want to hide, but I know that I have to do my presentation tomorrow, or "I feel sad and I hope it is because the relationship is going to break my heart."

Allowing is a process where the person enables the emotion to be present without trying to change or eliminate it immediately. In essence, this represents a significant shift in the person's mentality, from suppressing emotions to acknowledging and making space for them in their mind. You might be saying: "It's alright to be nervous about this situation" or "It is good to be sad because this is the only way for me to let go of the loss."

Investigation includes scrutinizing the feeling by involving only curiosity, not judgment. What part of your body is that feeling happening in? What thoughts come along with it? What is this feeling trying to say? What do you need at this moment? This scrutiny is gentle and inquisitive, rather than logical or critical.

Non-identification refers to the recognition that, although you are feeling the emotion, you are not the emotion itself. For instance, one could say: "I'm experiencing anxiety" instead of "I am anxious." This minor change of wording, in fact, separates the emotion from the speaker and prevents emotions from "winning" over the entire identity. At this point, some people may want to incorporate the element of Nurturing, which involves offering oneself the same kindness one would extend to a good friend experiencing similar troubles.

Distress Tolerance Skills

There are times when the emotions are so strong that the regulation methods seem completely inaccessible. At such times, distress tolerance skills are there to support you through the storm without the risk of the emotions getting worse by impulsive actions or self-destructive behaviors.

Distraction means temporarily shifting the focus away from dominant feelings to allow them to decline gradually. Successful distractions actually pull all of your attention in, and this can be through complex mental tasks, physical activities, creative pursuits, or social interactions. The trick is not to pick activities just to avoid emotions, but rather to select those that truly engage you.

Self-soothing is a process through which an individual uses their senses to calm themselves when overwhelmed by negative emotions. For instance, one might choose to listen to relaxing music, take a nice, warm bath, hold a familiar and comfortable object, look at the most beautiful pictures, or breathe in pleasant fragrances. No one can create their own self-soothing kit, as it will be unique and depend on individual preferences and what they feel is truly soothing.

Opposite Action is a technique that involves doing the complete opposite of what intense emotions desire, especially when those desires are not helpful in the current situation. For example, if anxiety is making you want to avoid a challenging but essential situation, the opposite action might involve moving toward it slowly and mindfully. Or if depression is making you isolate, the opposite action might include reaching out to others despite not feeling like it.

Radical Acceptance means taking reality as it is, even if it's painful or not what you want. This does not mean approving or liking the situation, but rather acknowledging what is true without wasting energy resisting or fighting against it. Most of the time, radical acceptance leads to less suffering because a large part of the pain comes from holding on to what is rejected in the already happening.

Cognitive Strategies for Emotional Resilience

The cognitive strategies for anxiety discussed in Chapter 5 represent only one side of the story; the other side involves additional cognitive approaches that specifically support emotional resilience across all emotional experiences.

Temporal Perspective means consciously choosing the time frame when describing the effect of a given event on your perspective. When emotions are too strong, it is better to consider how we will feel about this situation a week, a month, or even a year from now. This change of perspective does not diminish the current pain but frames it in a way that prevents the feelings from being permanent and all-encompassing.

Values-Based Decision Making refers to the process of making decisions based on your core values, regardless of what your emotions may tell you. When anxiety makes you avoid, the question you should ask yourself is: What action of mine would be most in tune with my values of growth, connection, or authenticity? On the other hand, if anger is driving you to say something hurtful, then think about what kind of reaction would be most in line with your values of compassion and integrity.

Story Revision acknowledges that you are continually creating stories about your life, and these stories largely shape the emotional reactions you experience. When dealing with problems, always try different stories consciously: Instead of "This only happens to me, I have no luck," put "This is a temporary setback that I can gain insight from." Instead of "I can't do this," think "It is difficult, and I am learning how to deal with difficult situations."

Psychological flexibility is the ultimate form of emotional resilience, the ability to adjust your reactions according to the environment's conditions while remaining true to your values and goals. Those who are psychologically flexible can navigate the most unbearable emotional cases without letting these emotions control them. They adjust their tactics when the current ones are not yielding results and continue moving forward even in the most challenging times.

A significant part of the rigidity in the psychological framework stems from the struggle against the unfortunate aspects of human life—difficult emotions, uncertainty, imperfection, and loss. The concept of psychological flexibility refers to maintaining awareness of life's realities while taking actions that bring you closer to the goals that matter most to you.

It is different, however, from total surrender to the forces of fate or downplaying one's right to change what is wrongly done. The latter, however, involves identifying what is within your sphere of control, accepting what cannot be changed, and simultaneously working vigorously on what is within your influence.

In practice, identify what parts of the challenging situation are under your influence, and which parts you have to accept. In any difficult situation, one is usually in control of their responses, preparation, attitude, and actions, and must consider the external outcomes, others' reactions, and the overall context of the situation.

Values-Based Living

One can become stronger through adversity by committing to the values they cherish most and adhering to them, no matter how challenging the situation becomes. These are the standards that define our understanding of right and wrong, and as such, dictate the choices we make throughout our lifetime. Even if the world around changes drastically, values stay the same and thus provide a sense of stability during the "emotional storms".

Survey life themes that are most important to you, and you will easily find out the core values that are yours. There are numerous examples of common value categories, such as relationships, growth, creativity, service, authenticity, security, adventure, spirituality, and achievement. Specific values within these groups will be exclusive to you.

Moreover, when dealing with challenging and unpleasant matters, make use of your values to guide you through the decision. Set the question: "What action would best agree with my values in such a case?" An action in line with one's values often requires bravery because it may contradict immediate emotional impulses or social pressures; however, long-term satisfaction and resilience are the results that follow.

Defusion from Thoughts and Emotions
Emotional agility involves recognizing that you can feel differently about certain things you think and still not act in accordance with those thoughts. The process, referred to as defusion, involves identifying thoughts as part of mental events that are not necessarily true and recognizing feelings as fleeting moments that do not last forever.

Practice observing your thoughts as mental events by using language like "I'm having the thought that..." or "My mind is telling me that..." instead of treating thoughts as facts. Similarly, observe emotions as experiences you're having rather than states you are: "I'm experiencing anxiety" rather than "I am anxious."

This observational stance opens up the psychological space for a more conscious choice in how you respond to thoughts and emotions. In this scenario, you can still feel anxious about the presentation without being forced to quit the field, should avoidance conflict with your values.

Building Self-Compassion
Self-compassion represents a significant shift in how you approach your own challenges, mistakes, and imperfections. Most people who find themselves in these situations respond by excessively self-criticizing themselves, hoping that this will lead to improvement. On the contrary, research consistently shows that self-compassion is more effective than self-criticism in promoting resilience, growth, and emotional well-being.

Major Elements of Self-Compassion

Self-compassion involves three interrelated parts. Self-Kindness means treating yourself with the same compassion and understanding you would give a close friend who is going through similar hardships. Instead of harsh self-judgment when you make mistakes or encounter difficulties, self-kindness involves demonstrating empathy and engaging in supportive self-talk.

Mindfulness Common Humanity

Humanity as a whole recognizes that suffering, imperfection, and obstacles are an inescapable part of the shared human experience, rather than a person's failure. Instead of feeling that no one understands and you are all alone when you have a hard time, the commonality of humanity stops you. It shows you that the same people are in similar situations too, so you are not isolated but connected with others.

Mindfulness allows us to suppress less and express more. It involves recognizing the suffering present here and now, without becoming overwhelmed by it or pretending that it doesn't exist.

Practicing Self-Compassion

People's self-compassion can be nurtured through both specific moments and everyday, unstructured applications. The Self-Compassion Break plays a formal role, available whenever suffering or difficulty is noticed.

Firstly, acknowledge the suffering moment: This is a moment of difficulty, or This hurts. Secondly, identify the essence of suffering: "Difficulty is part of life" or "No human is free of challenges like this." Thirdly, give yourself support: "May I be the support I need," or "May I share the love I would give to another with myself."

Moreover, instead of speaking formally, individuals can use the exact words they would use when talking to a trusted friend when they are speaking to themselves. When you notice critical self-talk, pause for a moment and ask yourself: "What would be my reaction if I were the best friend of the person who has just told me this struggle?" Then you should be as kind to yourself as you would be to your friend.

Self-Compassion and Motivation

A sizable portion of the world's population seems concerned that self-compassion might lead to a decline in motivation or a state of complacency with the status quo. On the contrary, scientific research shows that self-compassion actually increases motivation because it reduces the fear of failure, which is at the root of procrastination or avoidance. If you understand that, regardless of the results, you will be kind to yourself, then you are the one who will take sensible risks and persevere through the struggle.

Self-compassion also opens the doors to learning from mistakes by providing psychological safety for identifying errors without the feeling of shame or self-attack. This honesty is the one that pulls the person forward, rather than justifying mistakes with defensive justifications or treating oneself too harshly, a practice that does not lead to positive change.

Post-Traumatic Growth

As a matter of fact, it is not the case that all the people who encounter hardships or experience trauma end up with post-traumatic stress disorder. But most of them develop post-traumatic growth - a shift to the positive, that may come even after tough struggles. Learning about this phenomenon can be very helpful, as it provides a sense of hope and guidance when the going gets tough.

Domains of Growth

The domains of post-traumatic growth refer to the areas in which individuals develop and grow after experiencing such traumatic events.

Appreciation of Life is about recognizing that even the most ordinary experiences have their value and that life is truly precious. The people who have undergone this kind of growth mostly talk about a heightened perception of life's beauty, an enhanced appreciation for minor pleasures, and a more profound love for people and things they had not even realized were part of their experience while they took them for granted.

Relating to Others might become more profound through an everyday ordeal, leading to increased empathy and a higher level of openness towards other people. Many people believe that the hardships they experienced not only helped them form more genuine connections with others but also made them more empathetic towards those in similar situations.

Personal Strength is often recognized from the experience of the successful completion of a challenging situation that you thought was beyond your capability. It is not about being invulnerable; however, it is about having confidence in your ability to handle tough times and uncertainty.

New Possibilities may zoom in on the case; a disaster prompts one to rethink priorities, values, and direction. By marrying the original way of thinking and discarding old ways of living, a crisis can pave the way for new life to emerge, as the initial downsides of the pandemic become seeds for new opportunities to grow.

Spiritual Development is typically a process of deepening the connection with the most remarkable and transcendent aspects of the human experience, such as meaning, purpose, or anything else beyond the ordinary that has a spiritual nature. This could be happening within the current spiritual framework or alongside a new spirituality and purpose.

Facilitating Growth

Although growth cannot be forced and is not experienced by everyone, the following strategies can help create a setting favorable for personal development.

Active Coping is the process of confronting issues head-on; thus, you deal with them directly and positively, rather than avoiding them. One may need the assistance of a therapist to talk out issues, allowing you to actually face the problem instead of running away. Other activities that can be considered include writing down one's problems and thoughts, gradually allowing the problem to enter one's mind, and so on.

Meaning-making is the process of immersing oneself in figuring out how difficult experiences fit into the broader narrative of one's life. Some activities people might engage in include journaling, seeking professional help, exploring the spiritual side, and having conversations with others who have had similar experiences.

Narrative Reconstruction involves deliberately, step-by-step, embodying an individual's most challenging experiences as part of a coherent life story characterized by both struggle and strength, loss and learning, and pain and growth.

Building Your Support Network

Emotional resilience cannot be isolated. Humans are social creatures by nature, and the quality of our connections has a significant impact on our emotional resilience. Creating and nurturing trusting relationships is a must for survival and long-term resilience.

Types of Support

Different forms of support serve various functions in the formation of resilience:

Emotional Support is a type of assistance that enables individuals to feel comfort, love, and reassurance in times of trouble. One aspect of this is that people who listen without judgment, show empathy, and help you feel understood and valued will be more effective.

Instrumental Support is the provision of practical assistance during hard times—of money, labor, resources, or through concrete problem-solving. This can include childcare support during a period of hardship, help with everyday tasks when sick, or practical advice on navigating difficulties.

Informational Support is a source of advice, guidance, and information that helps one understand and cope with difficult situations. The information can come from doctors, individuals who have held similar positions, or experts in the field.

Social Integration is the feeling of being part of a larger community and having regular, positive social contacts that provide a sense of belonging and shared identity.

Cultivating Supportive Relationships

Building supportive relationships is a time- and energy-consuming task that requires deliberate actions and mutual effort. Authenticity means sharing your authentic self with the people in your life, rather than hiding behind a mask of perfection, even when you are struggling. The truthful interactions invite others to respond in kind, allowing the roots to grow deeper.

Active Listening

While others share their experiences, it fosters trust and reciprocity in relationships. Practice by giving others your full attention, repeating what you hear, and offering comfort without immediately offering advice.

Reliability means being consistently available within your capacity and fulfilling commitments. Often, these small, consistent acts of kindness are what build stronger relationships rather than the big ones.

Boundaries are part of a paradox that allows you to give in a way that is both sustainable and in a relationship without the other party feeling overwhelmed or resentful. Setting boundaries on what is and is not your responsibility helps maintain healthy relationships over time.

Professional Support

The importance of care cannot be overemphasized in personal relationships. However, professional support can provide critical knowledge and impartiality that friends and family cannot offer. The involvement of mental health professionals, spiritual advisors, coaches, and support groups can provide various forms of aid in building resilience. The presence of professional support is particularly vital if one is suffering from trauma, chronic mental health conditions, substance use, or other complicated issues that require specialized intervention.

Resilience Practices

Emotional resilience growth depends on habitually exercising the skills and perspectives that sustain one's psychological flexibility and emotional wellness.

Daily Resilience Practices

Gratitude Practice involves regularly acknowledging the positive experiences of a person, even when the situation is challenging. It does not necessarily mean that one has to ignore their problems, but rather, it is about being conscious of both what is working and what is challenging at the same time. The regular gratitude practice turns one's focus to the positive, i.e., the aspects that build psychological resources, which help resilience during difficult times.

Mindfulness Meditation helps one gain awareness of the present moment and acceptance, which is the basis for psychological flexibility. Even a short daily practice can lead to significant improvement in one's emotional regulation and reduce reactivity to challenging situations.

Physical Exercise not only helps alleviate stress but also, through the confidence-building experiences gained, the energy from the exercise session can be translated into greater emotional resilience. The regular physical challenges will continually build your confidence in handling discomfort and difficulty.

Creative Expression, when one opens up to the world through art, music, writing, or other creative outlets, not only involves emotional processing but also results in positive engagement, which in turn builds psychological resources.

Learning and Growth Activities keep a person psychologically flexible by actively seeking out new experiences and challenges, which not only push them out of their comfort zone but also expand their capabilities.

Weekly and Monthly Practices
Relationship nurturing involves maintaining contact with those people who matter most in your life, being true to yourself with them, and offering support to others.

Values Reflection is a periodic check to ensure one's behavior aligns with their core values, and making adjustments if a gap is noticed between values and behaviors.

A challenge review is about overcoming recent difficulties by identifying what was done well, what could have been improved, and what one has learned from the experience.

Future Visioning is already feeling relief and joy, receiving assistance, energy, and resources from hope and goals during tough times.

Integrating Resilience into Daily Life
The main aim is to incorporate resilience activities that can be done at any time during the day, making them the default reaction to problems instead of efforts that one has to remember to execute.

Environmental Supports

Redesign your environment so that it becomes your source of resilience:

Make areas that are peaceful and full of energy

Let the people and things that represent your values, strengths, and support network be around you

Some programs incorporate activities that build resilience

If possible, reduce the number of stressors in the environment

Proactive Resilience Building

Instead of waiting for a crisis to do so, be actively involved in regular practices to build up your psychological resources. Act out small scenarios to manage daily challenges, and then tackle bigger ones with confidence. Be always intently involved in the things that truly matter to your soul. During breaks and relaxed times in your life, strive to cultivate strong relationships that will provide support in times of trouble.

Continue learning throughout your life to ensure you remain mentally flexible.

Crisis Preparation

Work out very exact plans about your reactions and actions in challenging moments:

Be familiar with the circumstances that can be the first symptoms that you are going to be overwhelmed

Come up with a list of things to do that you are good at to help you get through different situations

Sign up your support network that will be ready to hear from you when it is time for a difficult phase of your life

Practice practical resources that help you during times of crisis

The Ongoing Journey

Making psychological resilience your goal is a lifelong experience, not an event. Various challenges will test your resilience, and you will continue to learn and grow throughout your life. This is the ordinary and expected way, not a failure-type reaction.

Your life will go through stages that will put more pressure on your resilience than on others. Major life transitions, deaths, health issues, and other significant sources of stress will test your coping abilities. These challenging times are opportunities to become more resilient than before, rather than merely indicators of the extent of one's previous growth.

Keep in mind that the quality of one's inner strength is not about making one robust or wiping out all kinds of mental pains from one's life. It refers to the process of becoming skilled in dealing with the challenges one meets in life, having the power to bounce back faster even after being dealt with severely, and still finding it worth practicing and being connected to the ultimate cause of life even when going through hard times Resilience skills and perspectives—emotional awareness, regulation strategies, psychological flexibility, self-compassion, supportive relationships, and growth-oriented practices, will be with you your whole life. They not only form a base for anxiety management but also offer a 'haven' for overall psychological well-being and life satisfaction.

While you are on your journey to building up resilience, give yourself the time to grow and feel the progress. Do not forget that the development of resilience is primarily achieved through repetitive daily exercises, rather than sudden breakthroughs.

Every time you act with consciousness instead of losing control to reactivity, you become worthy of compassion rather than criticism, and you are also living closer to your values during tough times.

When to Seek Support from Professionals

The Strength in Seeking Help

One of the central persistent myths about anxiety coping and building mental health strength is that it is a must to handle all scenarios by oneself. This myth leads to the conclusion that seeking help from a professional could be interpreted as a sign of weakness, failure, or inability. On the contrary, recognizing when you need a professional's support and taking action accordingly demonstrates that you are aware of your limitations, have the bravery to seek help, and take good care of yourself.

Thinking about anxiety and how Maria mastered it with her own, the first thing we see is the way she tried to help herself thoroughly: using diversification of methods, reading books on the subject, and so forth. It was some time before she could call off this inner struggle and tried the last, but successful, remedy - professional help. After about a year and a half of feeling increasingly anxious and experiencing panic attacks, she resorted to therapy. She was at her last resort, so finally her mental condition started to give way to self-pity, and she started to feel she was the problem.

When Maria was at last a therapist's client, she realized that her anxiety was due to the traumatic event of the car crash three years ago, which she had never really talked about or thought of. Through the professional assistance, she understood and mastered the most effective ways of confronting and overcoming the trauma, which were not found in the general anxiety self-help resources. As a result of her combined therapy and medication management, she has returned to normal and can live her life to the fullest in six months.

According to Maria, several key elements of her story, such as knowledge and strategies that can only be gained from professionals and not through self-help, are a point of strength rather than weakness when the subject of help arises. Additionally, several mental health issues are distinctly treatable via executed clinical intervention by trained professionals, as mentioned.

Professional support does not substitute for your personal efforts in managing anxiety, but instead supports them. The skills you have acquired through this book remain highly valuable and essential.

The professional help offers more methods, outlooks, and support that can make your advancement faster, as well as open the facets of anxiety that are difficult to handle alone.

Identifying the Need for Professional Help

One of the most challenging aspects of deciding to seek professional help is watching the borderline between ordinary anxiety and the anxiety that requires the intervention of a specialist - in some cases, this line may even be invisible. Anxiety is a phenomenon that can be found along a continuum, and what is considered problematic anxiety may change depending on the person and even the situation, based on individual circumstances, beliefs, and personal life demands.

Indicators of Severity and Duration

The presence of several such factors means that professional help would be beneficial:

Persistent Interference with Daily Functioning: The consistent anxiety that has a severely negative impact on your capacity to work, go to school, maintain relationships, take care of yourself, or do things you like is the time when professional support is very much needed. Maybe you are focusing so much on avoiding the moments you may have to do a presentation at work, thus hindering your career growth, and you are missing social events crucial to you, or you feel so overwhelmed with worry that you can't even complete your daily routine.

Duration and Lack of Improvement: If the anxiety that you have been going through for several weeks or months has not reduced and, in fact, it has worsened, then no matter how many self-management attempts you make, professional help should be sought out to receive new perspectives and techniques. Experiencing anxiety during a period of stress in life is normal; however, when the anxiety continues, and it does not respond to the self-management strategies, then it is likely that the intervention of a professional will be the most beneficial.

Escalating Symptoms:

If anxiety symptoms are worsening and not getting better with time, or if you get new symptoms, then the professional evaluation can suggest a more intensive therapy. The examples might be an increased number of panic attacks, wider avoidance behavior, or, at the same time, physical symptoms that make living difficult.

114

Physical Impact of Anxiety:

Long-term anxiety may lead to various illnesses such as heart diseases, stomach problems, sleep disorders, and immune system failure. If you have physical symptoms that may be due to anxiety, a medical evaluation can clarify the situation and the treatment.

Functional Impairment Areas

When a person's anxiety is so overwhelming that it adversely affects various aspects of life, they should comprehensively consider seeking professional help.

Work or Academic Performance:

Some examples include losing your attention during a conference call, which can remind you of times when you had to deal with professional people. Now you are hesitating to make contact because of anxiety, you may also be procrastinating on personal or work projects, just because of anxiety, and academic performance may go down, along with test anxiety or fear of meeting new people.

Relationships:

If you are not going to the places where society is gathering because of anxiety, are you constantly asking others for certainties, distancing yourself from the people you love, or is your anxiety a cause of family or friendship conflict, then most probably anxiety is the cause of the relationship strain.

Self-Care and Daily Activities:

There is always the issue of anxiety forcing one to neglect self-care activities such as regular eating, sleeping, and personal hygiene, and discouraging them from doing the necessary daily tasks. In such cases, professional support has the capacity to bring back these basic functions.

Personal Growth and Goals: Anxiousness that leads to putting off or abandoning your ambitions for the things that matter most to you in the areas of education, career, creativity, or even just your own self, etc., is one of the primary reasons why one should seek professional help, since a person will be given several excellent strategies to use for them to progress even when all the anxiety is ablaze in their minds.

Specific Symptom Indicators

There are a few specific symptoms or experiences that by themselves might be enough to make a person see a professional.

Panic Attacks: Typically, when one experiences a panic attack, they can sometimes manage it with self-help techniques. However, professional assistance can provide more specialized interventions that not only reduce the number but also the intensity. And this is primarily when the panic attacks, among other things, lead to a substantial avoidance of behavior, which, in turn, causes a low quality of life.

Obsessive Thoughts or Compulsive Behaviors: Intrusive thoughts that are distressing and hard to control, or repeated actions that seem necessary but interrupt daily life, are common issues that often improve with specialized professional treatments.

Trauma-Related Anxiety: If your anxiety is such that you can link it to a traumatic experience or situation so that it would seem like it came along with the trauma, then professional trauma treatment is the only way to go for safe recovery. The different trauma symptoms and mental health problems resulting from trauma are treated by trauma-informed therapy that has been specifically designed as such.

Suicidal Thoughts: Every single thought that relates to self-harm or suicide needs professional help without any delay at all. Don't be shy to ask for help if you ever experience such sensations by contacting a mental health crisis line, rushing to the nearest emergency department, or calling emergency services if suicidal thoughts attack you.

Substance Use: If you indulge in alcohol consumption, drug usage, or any other type of substance to help you manage anxiety, then the best solution would be for the professionals to cater to both the underlying anxiety and the substance use patterns. Anxiety and substance use frequently get intertwined to such an extent that specialized treatment approaches become necessary to unravel them.

Types of Mental Health Professionals

Mental health professionals come in different forms, and understanding their profiles may help you in picking out the best.

These are the different categories of professionals, categorized according to their educational background, the volume of knowledge they have acquired, the area of expertise, and the scope of their activities.

Psychologists

Clinical psychologists hold doctoral degrees in psychology and receive extensive training in psychological assessment and psychotherapy. They are capable of performing psychological evaluations that are of high quality, as well as diagnosing mental issues and providing different types of therapy. In addition to that, Psychologists cannot prescribe medications, but, for the most part, work cooperatively with psychiatrists or other medical providers when medication might be of assistance.

Furthermore, they approach patients with different disorders, such as anxiety, by which they train themselves and clients alike, in cognitive-behavioral therapy skills, or they work with ages like teenagers, Adolescents, or aged adults. E.g., they would have had an intensive proper training background for the use of the methodology in anxiety treatment and could provide you with the specialized therapy that is indescribable by your branch's general-purpose psychological counseling.

Psychiatrists

Psychiatrists are medical doctors who have completed medical school and have chosen to specialize in the field of mental health. They are the ones who give you the medications you need, check your physical health to see if the symptoms are due to it, and, in many cases, they are the ones who carry out the therapy sessions as well. The role of the psychiatrists becomes more solid when it comes to cases of biological factors, along with medication, when the anxiety is complex or when there is a physical and mental health relationship that is complicated.

Firstly, some psychiatrists are only concerned with medication management; however, there are also those who, besides medication, provide psychotherapy as well. Child and adolescent psychiatrists are a few who have extra training for dealing with children.

Licensed Professional Counselors (LPCs), Licensed Clinical Social Workers (LCSWs), Marriage and Family Therapists (MFTs), and other master's-level mental health practitioners provide talk therapy services. These experts each hold a master's degree in their respective fields and have undergone specialized training in providing therapy for a range of mental health-related concerns.

A significant part of anxiety can be treated by various licensed therapists who are exceptionally dedicated to this case and who may provide the necessary evidence-based treatments. They usually have a lot more openings than psychiatrists or psychologists, and thus can offer more appointment slots.

Psychiatric Nurse Practitioners

Psychiatric Mental Health Nurse Practitioners (PMHNPs) are advanced-degree nurses who, after specialized training in mental health, can prescribe medications, conduct psychiatric evaluations, and, in most cases, also provide psychotherapy. PMHNPs efficiently utilize their resources and can ensure comprehensive mental health care.

Primary Care

Even though primary care doctors cannot be considered as mental health specialists, they are, however, in a position to make the first assessment of the condition and, if the patient is anxious, to prescribe anxiety medication that is commonly used. They can then refer a patient to an appropriate mental health resource in case the anxiety becomes severe. They are, thus, usually the first people whom one can contact when anxiety treatment is sought and, therefore, can help ensure that there is a smooth flow of care between mental and physical health practitioners.

Evidence-Based Treatments for Anxiety

The treatment of anxiety through professional mental health care allows you to access those interventions that are based on solid evidence and scientific proof for their effectiveness in treating anxiety. Knowing these treatments may help you decide if you need a professional's help and anticipate the results of therapy.

Cognitive-Behavioral Therapy (CBT)

CBT is ranked among the most successful and well-documented anxiety disorders treatment trials. The principle of the therapy is to demonstrate the interconnections among thoughts, feelings, and behaviors, leading to an increase in thoughts that maintain anxiety.

Generally, anxiety-related CBT attempts to cover the following areas: Psychological education on anxiety provides information about what anxiety is, its causes, and its impact on both the body and the mind. Such information pacifies the drive for anxiety, which is very often the fear and confusion that accompany anxiety symptoms.

Cognitive Restructuring is a process that involves identifying and disputing anxious thoughts, generating more balanced thoughts, and continually assessing the validity and helpfulness of these thoughts.

Behavioral Interventions involve exposure to feared situations by overcoming the fear step by step, scheduling activities to increase participation in valued activities, and conducting behavioral experiments to test the accuracy of anxious predictions.

Exposure Therapy is a part of CBT that deals explicitly with the method of gradually and systematically exposing the patient to the feared situation or sensations in a strictly controlled manner. The process leads to a reduction in avoidance behaviors, showing that the fears do not materialize as often or are much easier to overcome than expected.

Acceptance and Commitment Therapy (ACT)

ACT is centered on empowering mental flexibility. This is the mind's ability to perceive current reality through values and thought, allowing it to act, even if the feelings are complicated. That is why, in the case of anxiety, the therapy doesn't seek to make the patient get rid of it, but to help the latter to have a different state of mind, distinct from the one currently existing, of troubled thoughts and feelings.

ACT strategies also include moment awareness skills, life values revelation activities, and taking actions consistent with one's values, even when anxiety is present. This method may be very beneficial to those persons who, in an attempt to rid themselves of anxiety, have exhausted all control strategies but have not achieved any results.

Dialectical Behavior Therapy (DBT)

DBT was initially conceptualized for the treatment of patients who had emotional regulation difficulties, but has been further developed for the treatment of anxiety disorders. The therapy is designed to create the following four skill sets: mindfulness, distress tolerance, emotion regulation, and interpersonal effectiveness.

DBT techniques could be very beneficial to individuals whose anxiety is accompanied by raging feelings, self-harming practices, or troubled relationships with other people.

Eye Movement Desensitization and Reprocessing (EMDR)

EMDR is a method of therapy for cases of trauma-related anxiety and post-traumatic stress disorder. The treatment consists of re-experiencing the traumatic incident while doing bilateral stimulation (usually eye movements), so the brain can process the trauma more adaptively.

EMDR can be one of the best methods to treat anxiety if it is the case of a specific traumatic event, or the symptoms that cause anxiety are a result of past traumatic experiences.

Medication Options

Anxiety medication, in most cases, is not necessary; however, it can be beneficial for some people, either as a single intervention or as a combination with therapy.

Selective Serotonin Reuptake Inhibitors

(SSRIs) They are the first that come to the mind of doctors when patients with anxiety disorders are in question. By elevating serotonin levels in the brain, these drugs not only alleviate anxiety but also depressive symptoms that usually accompany the situation.

Some widely used SSRIs are sertraline, fluoxetine, and escitalopram. Serotonin-Norepinephrine Reuptake Inhibitors (SNRIs) such as venlafaxine and duloxetine target both serotonin and norepinephrine systems and, thus, can stand as a suitable option in cases of anxiety disorders.

Benzodiazepines such as lorazepam, clonazepam, and alprazolam are capable of providing the patient with fast and effective relief from anxiety. Still, they can only be used for a limited period and at low doses due to the development of tolerance and risk of dependence. After a brief time, they are usually discontinued and replaced with long-term solutions.

Beta-blockers such as propranolol might be instrumental in controlling the somatic symptoms of anxiety attacks, especially in situations where the person is going to perform in front of others. These drugs do not have any direct effect on anxiety thoughts and feelings, but they can alleviate symptoms such as palpitations and shaking.

Other medications like gabapentin, hydroxyzine, and a few antipsychotics might be considered as an auxiliary choice for the treatment of anxiety disorders if the most effective methods fail or if the patient has a particular type of anxiety.

Specialized Treatments

Specific anxiety presentations can be improved with the help of specialized treatment approaches:

Intensive Outpatient Programs (IOPs) offer several hours of care per week and may be a good option in case of severe anxiety. They can be a valuable alternative to hospitalization in case of extreme anxiety that substantially interferes with the proper functioning of the patient.

Partial hospitalization Programs are designed to treat patients full-time while still allowing them to sleep at home. These programs usually maintain a good level of contact with the family and the community and intend to bring down the levels of severe anxiety.

Residential Treatment is a program that offers care for individuals who are experiencing anxiety that is treatment-resistant and that is so severe that their functioning is significantly impaired. These programs, as a rule, last only a short time and focus more on the phase of stabilization and intensive skill building.

Support Groups managed by mental health professionals may not only provide expert guidance but also the support of peers. Sometimes, these groups can be especially effective in the case of a specific type of anxiety or occurrence in life.

The Way to the Best Professional

The choice of a mental health professional should not be taken lightly, as it is a milestone that can significantly impact the treatment, affecting not only its efficiency but also your mood and motivation. Your choice can be based on several considerations.

Practical Considerations

Insurance Coverage: Ensure you understand what type of mental health assistance your insurance will cover. Be mindful of copays, deductibles, and referral requirements. Some insurance plans have a limited list of providers that you can access while covered under them, and others give you more flexibility.

Location and Accessibility

"Location: First, think about whether you would be most comfortable with an in-person or telehealth service, and find out if the location of your chosen provider is suitable for you to get there. Telehealth is now highly accessible and can be a good option for individuals who are hesitant to leave their homes or travel to appointments.

Scheduling Availability: Some providers have lengthy waiting lists, while others offer more immediate availability. Think about how sensitive your desire for treatment is and whether you are ready to wait for a specific therapist, if so.

Cost: If you are paying for yourself or have a high deductible, focus on the service fees and check if the providers offer a sliding scale of fees or installment plans.

Professional Qualifications

Licensing and Credentials: Ensure that any provider you consider is appropriately licensed in your state and possesses the necessary credentials for their profession. Most licensing boards maintain online databases that allow you to verify provider licenses.

Specialization in Anxiety: Search for a provider who is not only a general therapist but is specifically trained in anxiety disorders by adding the said area as a skill to their profile. Specialized training and experience in anxiety treatment can significantly impact treatment effectiveness.

Evidence-Based Practice: Utilize the services of medical professionals who specialize in evidence-based therapies, such as CBT, ACT, EMDR, or other methods with scientific backing for the treatment of anxiety disorders.

Training and Experience: Review the provider's qualifications, including the number of years in practice and their specific experience with your type of anxiety or life circumstances.

Personal Fit Factors

Therapeutic Relationship: Your connection with the therapist is the topmost indicator of your treatment's success. In the early sessions, decide if you feel listened to, comprehended, and relaxed with

your provider.

Communication Style: A provider is a unique individual, and so are their communication methods. Some providers are more direct and organized, while others are more open and creative in their approach. Figure out which one can gain the most for you.

Cultural Competence: In case of culture-related factors being

Significant in your life, look for providers who demonstrate a high degree of understanding of and extensive experience with your cultural background, identity, or life circumstances.

Gender and Age: Some people prefer their healthcare professionals to be of the opposite gender, younger, or older than themselves, as they find comfort in this arrangement or believe these professionals can better relate to their experiences.

Questions to Ask Potential Providers

Please consider asking this when thinking of a new provider:

What is your experience in treating anxiety disorders specifically?

What treatment approaches do you use for anxiety?

What is the treatment process like, and how long does it typically take?

How do you assess treatment progress?

If there is a crisis, can I contact you between sessions?

Do you collaborate with other healthcare professionals to develop a care plan or provide me with additional support?

What are your fees and payment policies?

What to Expect from Professional Treatment

One of the ways to make professional anxiety treatment less frightening and to facilitate the treatment in which you are engaged is to understand what to expect.

First-Time Evaluation

The initial visits usually include a thorough evaluation of the anxiety symptoms, their history and development, current lifestyle, previous treatment, and your aims for therapy.

Your doctor will probably cover the following topics in detail:

When your anxiety symptoms began and how they've changed over time

Specific situations that trigger your anxiety

How anxiety affects different aspects of your life

What you have done to lower anxiety levels (including what has worked and what has not)

Your medical history and current medications

Family history of anxiety or other mental health conditions

Current life stressors and support systems

Your strengths, resources, and coping strategies

This assessment process helps your provider understand your unique situation and develop an appropriate treatment plan.

Treatment Planning

After the evaluation, your provider will combine your treatment goals with detailed interventions to create a personalized treatment plan.

Definition of the main issues through goals and objectives

Recommended treatment approaches

Expected timeline for treatment

How progress will be measured

Any referrals to other providers if needed

A provider is likely to accept a sliding-scale fee based on the clients' incomes.

The public center for infants' guidance is accustomed to providing low-cost services.

Some companies have long-term employee assistance programs that assure free short-term counseling.

Online therapy resources are likely to present a more affordable therapeutic pathway.

Group therapy usually has a cheaper price than individual therapy

University training clinics for supervised trainees typically provide services at a highly discounted rate

Telehealth options that eliminate the need for transportation

Providers who offer services during the evening and weekend

Employee assistance programs, which can be a source of services at work for you

Friends or family who would be willing to look after your children while you go to the doctor

Intensive formats, which involve fewer total appointments

Get your family doctor to suggest some secondary doctors you could use to treat yourself

Ask a medical insurance firm to provide a list of doctors who are included, and you are covered when you go to them

Go through the provider directory that the professional organizations on the internet furnish

Ask friends and family members that you trust if they know anyone who can help you in such a situation

Reach out to the community-based mental health organization for support

Sharing with the therapist the instances of your life, which include experiences that might be embarrassing or shameful

Conducting "homework" assignments and skill rehearsals in between the therapy sessions

Asking questions when you didn't understand the topic

Offering feedback on what was effective and what was not

Trying new methods with a mindset that even if they make you feel uncomfortable, it won't last long

Realistic Expectations

Keep a realistic perspective on the whole therapy process:

Significant changes are made gradually, one step at a time, rather than all at once

You will likely be very uncomfortable when you try to avoid situations and feelings

Therapy that you do outside the sessions is vital, and the better part of the work is done in sessions

The moment setbacks happen, do not get depressed over them, as they are normal and do not indicate that the therapy process is not working.

Since different people respond differently to various treatment methods, you might be required to experiment with various techniques until the right one is found.

Communication with Your Provider

Communication via open channels with your provider is the key to efficiency in treatment:

Express not only your goals but also any problems and preferences that you may have related to the treatment

Continue to advise on your experience of different interventions

Explanations about the treatment requested by you

Mention your fear of the closeness of the relationship with the therapist.

Inform your therapist if you are thinking about ending therapy

Integration with Self-Care

The help from the professional is most effective when complemented by continuous good self-care:

The lifestyle habits that you talked about in Chapter 6 should be maintained

Keep building on your physical and cognitive exercises previously learnt in the book

Create and nurture relationships that give you the needed emotional support

Participate in the things that you find interesting and give you a sense of purpose

Try to be aware of and enjoy the small gains instead of waiting for one big leap forward

Accept that a relapse will not be the end of the process, but just a stage in it

Keep the emphasis on progress rather than on perfection

Don't forget that new skills will require time and effort before they become automatic

The inadequacy of the therapeutic approach to your specific anxiety is the leading cause of inefficient treatment

Other issues (trauma, depression, physical conditions) are completely taking over the stage, so that there is no room for anxiety release

The therapist-patient relationship might be less than ideal

You might be very stressed by things out of your control and not have enough energy left to make a change

The aims of the treatment may not be in line with what you hope for

Perhaps there is a need for a longer, more intense treatment program

Talking through your worries candidly with your present doctor

Inquiring about different treatment options

Getting a second opinion from another doctor

Reflecting on whether other related issues need to be dealt with

Determining if the condition has gotten worse and if more treatment is necessary

Thinking about whether medication would be an option if you have not used it before

Thoughts of self-harm or suicide

Severe panic attacks that do not alleviate with the usual coping strategies

Psychotic symptoms (hearing voices, seeing things that others do not, being very suspicious)

Severe dissociation, or when one feels completely separated from the world

Using substances in dangerous quantities as a means of dealing with anxiety

Not being able to take care of oneself or do the most basic everyday things

Understanding what you are going through
Offering the right kind of help

Not allowing them to cause your anxiety to get worse unintentionally

Understanding your needs and helping you to cope when things are not going well

Feeling less anxious about your situation

You are the one who gets to choose how much information about your treatment is going to be revealed.

Friends and family who may be doing it with good intentions should never take on the role of your therapist.

Apart from your advice, nobody's opinion about your treatment should be the reason for you to stop the care you receive from a professional

It is you who has the power to ask for the kinds of support that you need and even refuse some.

Relationships are greatly impacted by anxiety

Family dynamics give rise to anxiety patterns

Your family members are having a hard time understanding and supporting your recovery

Relationship issues are contributing to your anxiety

Long-Term recovery and maintenance

Usually, professional treatment of anxiety is acute, and there is also

a phase for long-term maintenance.

Definition of Recovery

The first thing that recovery from anxiety does not mean is the complete eradication of the anxiety-mumbled feelings that are a part of it, and that would be neither realistic nor healthy. Correspondingly, recovery may mean:

Symptoms of anxiety that do not impact daily life much

Trust that you can cope with the anxiety situation if it happens

The continuation of what you have been doing in terms of activities and relationships that are of value to you

Building up the most effective coping mechanisms for you

Acceptance of your anxiety-related habits and triggers

Maintenance Strategies

Keeping the improvements after professional treatment, mostly, requires the following actions:

Skills that were acquired in treatment are kept practicing

To identify the onset of anxiety, self-observation is conducted regularly

Regular and continuous contact with your mental health professional.

Practicing a healthy lifestyle is detrimental to mental health.

Preparing for stressful events and unexpected moments in life involves having a plan.

Preventing Relapse

An example of a relapse of anxiety is that it may happen during stressful life periods. The prevention of relapse refers to:

Learning the personal signs that show that your anxiety is on the rise.

It is a must to make a list of activities that one can do in case of anxiety.

Keeping in contact with mental health professionals so that the reinstatement of therapy is swift in case of necessity

Being consistent in the use of the tools, approaches, and lifestyles that have been beneficial

Don't feel disappointed if you need more professional help in the future.

The Integration of Professional and Personal Resources

The most successful paradigm of anxiety management typically combines professional treatment with patient self-care, peer and family support, as well as lifestyle adjustments.

Professional treatment offers:

Expertise and specialization
Uptake of the main clinical issues through research and practice
An arm of the decision-making process
The earliest and easiest access to help during a crisis
Pharmaceutical remedies, if necessary

Personal resources supply:

Regular and lived-through instances of management abilities

Lifestyle cornerstones that nurture mental health

Friends to talk to and socialize with

Interest and enjoyment in living the daily life

Continued stabilization of progress

Along with the collaboration of the profession-specific modality and client-centered engagement, it forms the most complete apparatus for the successful management of anxiety and for the long-term abstinence from symptoms.

Moving Forward with Confidence

If it were your decision, I bet you would have chosen one of the ways to help you now, but the irony is that you have decided to go for professional help, which is the best thing to do. It is an act of bravery that demonstrates your value for your mental health and willingness to continue investing in it, although the returns will mostly not be immediate.

Always remember that asking for help demonstrates wisdom, not power. Just as you would take a doctor's advice and consult an expert in the case of a severe physical health problem, you should do the same with anxiety if it has a substantial negative impact on your life.

It is a process of anxiety management that needs professional help. The therapist is an excellent source of knowledge, perspective, and encouragement. With the help of experts, your personal dedication, and the exercises outlined in this book, you are equipped with the resources to lead a successful life free from anxiety.

Firstly, note that anxiety, to some extent, is not necessarily a bad thing, and it should not be a perpetual source of your identity. On the other hand, it need not define you, stop you from achieving your best, or dictate your future. However, through a combination of professional help and personal efforts, the skills and strength needed to face and overcome life's problems will develop. Easy as it is, in the long run, the decision to seek professional help, when necessary, will be one of the best investments you can make in your mental and general health.

As a matter of fact, the more you are going to be anxious in certain situations along the way, the more it will be possible to build self-confidence and personal growth to exist side by side. The point of recovery from anxiety is that it is always possible, and help is always there for you; thus, you are worthy of a life without constant anxiety. Suppose you are a beginner seeking professional help, or a mental health provider who has been guiding patients for some time. In that case, the same thing is true for all of them: progress is the best thing you can achieve by taking every step in the right direction—walking towards better mental health.

Correct me if I am wrong, but the methods, different points of view, and knowledge one can gain from reading this book and discussing it with a therapist or psychologist, even for a short time, eventually foster a holistic approach to anxiety management as well as a deep understanding of oneself. Personal dedication to the process of self-understanding, finding effective coping mechanisms, cultivating inner strength, and seeking help when needed is a testament to one's courage and a smart move towards better mental health.

Spiritual and Philosophical Approaches

Exploring Meaning, Purpose, and Faith as Supports Against Anxiety. Amid anxiety's turbulent waves, the desire for more profound and meaningful experiences keeps many individuals away from the conventional therapy methods and medications. They seek vehicles of sense-making that transcend the immediate problems of palpitations, overwhelming thoughts, and disabling fear. Such extensive searching mainly results in an extraordinary experience and philosophy, which people have turned to for centuries in times of uncertainty and misery.

The conjunction of spiritual and philosophical ideas with human psychological conditions is ancient and at the same time very much modern in dealing with the cases of anxiety. Situation-wise, the whole concept moves us from the likes of Stoic philosophers of ancient Rome era, who were the first to develop methods for worry management, to various Buddhist meditation techniques that teach the acceptance of life's uncertainty, and then further to modern existential sets that are convincing individuals to create a sense of meaning when faced with the absurdity of life. The root of the issue is common to all these varying traditions. They address it differently, with many complementing and even sometimes outperforming purely psychological approaches in their transcendental nature when compared side by side.

The goal of this article is to open up new horizons of thought and spiritual experience, and to welcome such frameworks into our lives as a help, not by removing unpleasant feelings or situations, but by providing explanations, a voice, and practices that change how we relate to the unknown and suffering. Consequently, the reader will be invited to study choirs and traditions, from well-established global religions to non-religious philosophical movements, always keeping their practical application in daily life in focus.

First and foremost, spiritual and philosophical views of anxiety should be considered as supports that accompany professional mental health treatment, not as substitutes. Furthermore, they provide answers to the questions of meaning and purpose that often underlie anxious suffering. These methods concede that an anxiety disorder is not just a clinical condition to be controlled, but frequently an intense human experience that is suggestive of issues of living, meaning, and our location in the universe.

The Intersection of Spirituality and Anxiety

Through spirituality, which is essentially the search for a connection with a higher being than oneself, the human response has always been very close to the one, especially in times of anxiety and uncertainty. One of the leading causes of the emergence of spiritual communities is their response to the everyday anxieties inherent in the human condition: death, a sense of meaninglessness, solitude, and the unpredictable nature of life.

Anxiety, at most, can be seen as a loss of control and a crisis. The signs of danger to our lives, personality, or ability to foresee and navigate the future trigger our minds to enter an anxious mode. Spiritual methods do not address these questions by claiming authority over them or offering certainties; instead, they acknowledge the complexity of the issues. However, they are presenting us with different views on our relationship with the unknown.

Almost all spiritual traditions view anxiety as a normal reaction of the human body, which, although not pleasant, can be used as a sign of access to inner wisdom and a catalyst for growth beyond it. The term "nights of the soul" in Christianity refers to the spiritual anxiety and emptiness experienced during a period of spiritual growth, which can lead to a deeper faith. In addition, Islamic doctrine refers to anxiety as a challenge that brings one closer to Allah. According to Hindu belief, the anxious feeling is the root of all suffering (dukkha), which ultimately motivates the spiritual journey towards liberation.

This transformation, describing anxiety as a potential spiritual guide rather than only a negative symptom, is a fundamental perspective shift. Instead of seeing anxiety as an enemy that must be eradicated at any cost, the spiritual methods generally allow the exploration of the teaching's anxiety, which can help us understand our attachments, fears, and most hidden desires.

Among others, the spiritual concept of surrender present in various spirituality traditions is the most potent recourse to the anxiety's thirst for control. It is reflected in the Christian expression "letting go and letting God," the Muslim concept of "submission to Allah," and the Buddhist practice of "accepting the present moment." The core spiritual tactic here is the handling of one anxiety feature - the fruitless fight to master what cannot be learned - the struggle for control over the uncontrollable.

Ancient Wisdom: Stoicism and Anxiety Management

The Stoic philosophy, which originated in ancient Athens, was likely one of the most established systems in the ancient world, offering a comprehensive approach to anxiety treatment. The Stoic teachings, as presented in the works of Epictetus, Marcus Aurelius, and Seneca, do not lag; they continue to shed surprisingly contemporary light on the problem of anxiety and the best ways to regulate it.

Most anxiety is caused by our desire to manage situations, which, in the end, are beyond our control. We become anxious about futures that may never come, worry about what others might think of us, or get upset by situations that can't be changed. Employing stoicism means always going back to the question, "Can I control this thing?" If the answer is no, the stoic reaction is to accept and redirect the energy to the area where it can be most effectively influenced.

The Stoics use the term "negative visualization" to describe the practice of imagining the loss of the most valuable things in one's life. Habituating the mind to the idea of letting go and gaining serenity, rather than mounting anxiety. This is not done to cause more fear, but rather by visualizing and rehearsing the loss of the most valuable things, to gain detachment from the outcome and strengthen inner fortitude. By imagining the loss of what we cherish most, we become thankful for what we have and reduce the anxiety caused by the fear of losing it.

Contemporary cognitive-behavioral therapy (CBT) has generally drawn much of its material from Stoic philosophy, emphasizing that our thoughts about events, rather than the events themselves, are what primarily give rise to our feelings. Consequently, the Stoic method of scrutinizing and questioning our presumptions and judgments closely resembles the CBT approach for controlling intrusive thoughts.

Buddhist Perspectives on Anxiety and Suffering

Perhaps, among various spiritual frameworks, Buddhism is the one that provides the most detailed and extensive model for understanding and dealing with anxiety. It is built around the Four Noble Truths, which directly address the nature of suffering and the way to overcome it. The First Noble Truth confesses that suffering (dukkha) is the lot of human life, whereas the subsequent ones define the causes and outline the way that leads to release from the yoke of suffering.

Seen through the lens of Buddhism, anxiety is a symptom of dukkha that comes from the fact that we are totally wrong about the nature of reality. We suffer because we hold on to temporary things, try to find safety in a world that is by its very nature insecure, and keep telling ourselves that we are one and only. It is the same self that differs from others, which is why it must be looked after and defended.

The Second Noble Truth points to desire (tanha) as the leading cause of suffering. The source of anxiety is often the dependence on one or another possible development of events, the thirst for certainty and control over the situation, and the rejection of discomfort and change, which vie for the contradictory. The reason we get anxious is that we want things to be exactly the way we prefer and expect, and that is precisely when reality becomes a threat to our preferences and expectations.

Buddhist mindfulness practice provides the most direct way to address our anxious thoughts and sensations. Instead of struggling with anxiety or completely getting lost in its flow, the practice of mindfulness shows us how to witness the anxious experiences by using a delicate and impartial observation. It also lessens the identification with anxiety, which, in most cases, is the reason why anxious thoughts and feelings become more powerful.

The technique of noting, which is very typical in Vipassana meditation, involves recognizing the arising of anxious thoughts and sensations, and simultaneously labeling them as "Anxiety," "worrying," "tension," or "fear." By doing this, psychological distance is created, helping us see that we are not the anxiety, but rather the consciousness that can reckon it.

The instance of anxiety can become this Buddhist teaching of impermanence, a most helpful model for handling the disorder. Anxiety often consists of endlessly pushing current worries down the timeline into the future or grasping at past events as the only truths about the world. The acknowledgment that all things are constantly changing can bring a decrease in anxiety because it popularizes the fact that unpleasant situations, like everything else, are transient and are open to change.

The idea of "beginner's mind" is still another great source of viewpoint in dealing with anxiety. Most anxious thoughts are assumptions about what might happen, what has happened before, and what you fear may be true. A beginner's mind enables one to experience each moment with a fresh perspective, unencumbered by preconceived notions of how things are supposed to or will unfold.

Loving-kindness meditation is one of the most effective ways to counter self-critical thoughts, which are the most common companions of anxiety and also harsh judgment. When we cultivate compassion towards others and ourselves, the inner critic, which is the primary source of anxious suffering, will become weaker. The fundamental words of loving-kindness meditation—"May I be happy, may I be peaceful, may I be free from suffering"—are indeed a repelling force against the storm of harsh self-talk that anxiety holds.

The "Middle Way" teaching of the Buddha is invaluable in charting a course that avoids the two extremes: either absolute immersion in anxious thoughts and feelings or their complete suppression.

Practically, this matrimonial ceremony with anxiety is not about walking talk, nor about getting lost in it; it is rather a gentle touch of acknowledgment without either of the above reactions.

Christian Contemplative

Through prayer, meditation, and deep trust in divine providence, Christianity has shaped a landscape that would otherwise have been very different, with its vibrant, rich, and multifaceted contemplative traditions that address the problem of anxiety. Generally speaking, the Christian perspectives on anxiety have been quite different in various denominational and traditional settings; nevertheless, several recurring themes are identifiable. They not only serve as a source of relief and help but also constitute a sign of hope for people engrossed and trapped by anxious thoughts and feelings.

The primary and most explicit Jesus's point on the question of anxiety in the Sermon on the Mount is «Therefore do not worry about tomorrow, for tomorrow will worry about itself. Each day has its own troubles. This saying is the very nucleus of the fundamental Christian approach to anxiety, which, instead of fixation on future outcomes and the need to be in control, shifts the attention to present-moment trust and reliance on God's providence.

Through the different religious contexts of the world, the usage of prayer, which is one of the monastic spiritual exercises, is a significant way of dealing with anxiety issues. It is said that through Centering Prayer, made popular by the modern personage of Thomas Keating, one lets go of thoughts and anxiety by repeating a sacred word. This makes it possible for God to fill that space, allowing one to enter into a deeper union with God.

Lectio Divina, a tradition of meditating on the Bible, is another way to deal with anxiety through spiritual exercises. The process of Reading, Meditation, Prayer, and Contemplation enables people to feel the holy scriptures as a source of comfort and guidance. Often, they come across secrets that directly relate to their current anxieties and help them work through them.

The method of letting go, which is the keystone of a lot of Christian perspectives on anxiety, means that one should give up the delusion of control and entrust oneself to the plan of God. It does not indicate becoming inactive or failing to take the correct step when necessary; rather, it is about not being overly carried away by our efforts and being open to results that differ from our preferences.

Prayer itself tackles anxiety in several ways. Petitionary prayer allows individuals to express their concerns and request assistance, creating a sense of emotional relief and a feeling of being supported by a divine force. Prayers of thanksgiving move the focus from what is lacking or threatening to what is full and blessed. Meditative prayer develops the quiet within that can become a sanctuary against the onslaught of anxious ideation.

Moreover, the Christian community and fellowship are very close to the heart, and mental problems, things like isolation, are indeed less addressed.

The concept of providence, the belief that God is at the center of the world's situation and works for good even in times of adversity, serves as a model for understanding suffering and uncertainty in a way that reduces anxiety.

Islamic Approaches to Peace and Trust

The faith of Islam offers a holistic paradigm for overcoming anxiety, featuring the development of Tawakkul (trust in Allah) and the recognition of divine sovereignty over all affairs. The term "Islam" itself is derived from the root s-l-m in Arabic, which is connected to peace, submission, and surrender—concepts that reach the very core of anxiety and simultaneously provide avenues for its resolution.

The Quran mentions worry as one of the things that happens to people. Yet, it stills people's hearts: "And it is He who sends down rain after [people] have despairs and spreads His mercy. And He is the Protector, the Praiseworthy" (42:28). Such a verse, like many others, assures the believers that God's compassion and support are at their disposal even in their abyss and fear.

One of the ways to calm the nervous works of the mind is Dhikr (remembrance of Allah). The use of the faithful words (There is no power except with Allah) can be very helpful in taking the mind from worrying to the presence of God and His help. Besides this, the person can be anywhere and perform these tasks; they are free at that time, making them more accessible in moments of crisis or anxiety.

The five daily prayers (Salah) can be compared to a spiritual walk, during which one can find solace at any of the stopping points. The upheaval of the body, chanting of Quranic verses, and the bowing towards Mecca all contribute to the movement of the individual from his concerns to the vastness of the universe.

The Quranic teaching system firmly holds the view that Allah puts the believers through all sorts of trials, including anxiety and fear, and these trials would lead to spiritual purification and growth. The Quran mentions: "And We will surely test you with something of fear and hunger and a loss of wealth and lives and fruits, but give good tidings to the patient" (2:155). This point of view turns the anxiety back from being mere suffering into a potential spiritual opportunity.

The concept of Qadar (divine decree) establishes a paradigm that balances the acceptance of situations beyond one's control with the acknowledgment that individuals have the power to influence their actions.

Meditation in Islam differs significantly from other religious traditions as it is not a strict set of practices but revolves around the attributes of Allah, the understanding of His creation through the verses of the Quran, and the consciousness of divine presence in the heart. These activities not only lead to tranquil hearts but also put trust in the Almighty, which eventually becomes a powerful support against anxious thoughts and feelings.

In an environment where anxiety is the center of lamentation, the Islamic principle of Ummah (community) is a significant point that can convert solitariness, which is one of the critical effects of anxiety, into a community. Becoming a member of a congregation, joining support groups, and participating in religious activities practiced by others are ways to receive and offer support, which is known to reduce individual anxiety.

First of all, knowledge (Ilm) is extensively cherished in Islamic tradition. It involves not only spiritual realization but also the practical mastery of fear, anxiety, and worry through the use of spirituality. A lot of Islamic scholars have expounded in a very detailed manner about the anxiety treatment by the use of Islamic doctrines and practices.

Mindfulness

Anxiety is usually a condition where one is either dwelling on what happened in the past or imagining bad things that will happen in the future. By practicing mindfulness, one learns to train one's attention to remain present in the here and now. In the present, narratives about the past and future have significantly less value in alleviating anxiety. This is not about ignoring one's legitimate needs for planning or learning from past experiences, but rather about not getting caught up in anxious, repetitive thinking.

Mindfulness practice, which involves disengaging oneself from thoughts and refraining from using them as one's identity, creates a distance between the observer and anxious thoughts. Instead of saying "I am anxious," mindfulness offers the perspective, "I notice anxious thoughts coming." This slight distinction can make a significant difference in the intensity and duration of anxious episodes.

Physical awareness exercises are suitable for people to be able to figure out the early physical symptoms of anxiety that have not been turned into angry outbursts. By recognizing the physical manifestations of anxiety, such as shallow breathing and muscle tension, one can calm down more quickly by applying calming techniques.

Breath awareness serves as both the anchor and the instrument in a mindfulness practice. The breath is always available as a present-moment anchor, and conscious breathing exercises can activate the parasympathetic nervous system, providing direct relief from the physiological effects of anxiety.

Passing through self-criticism, the harsh inner voice, and self-doubt that usually appear together with anxiety, the technique of loving-kindness meditation can turn the situation upside down. By growing care for oneself and others, individuals may become less hostile with the inner environment where anxiety is spreading.

Walking meditation and mindful movement practices are alternatives to sitting meditation and, probably, more accessible when high anxiety and sitting still conflict. Although these practices remain faithful to mindfulness principles, they allow for a physical movement that can release the tension of anxious energy.

Informal mindfulness practices are ways of integrating awareness into daily activities. Mindful eating, walking, listening, and working can transform everyday activities into opportunities for present-moment awareness and anxiety reduction.

The process of RAIN (Recognition, Acceptance, Investigation, Natural awareness) is a system that helps the person to get through the challenging emotions, including anxiety. The Model guides the person through acknowledging anxious feelings, accepting them without judgment, exploring their characteristics with curiosity, and resting in the awareness that observes all experiences.

Mindfulness-Based Stress Reduction (MBSR) and Mindfulness-Based Cognitive Therapy (MBCT) are two of the most significant developments in mindfulness for medical settings. They facilitate interactive programs for individuals suffering from anxiety or depression. The scientific community has validated these methods thoroughly to lead to the successful treatment of patients' anxiety symptoms. Additionally, research has shown that these methods are effective in preventing relapse in patients.

One of the most influential principles in the world is the concept of "Meaning in Suffering". Among others, anxiety and suffering have been recognized as the starting point for growth, wisdom, and deeper understanding by most spiritual and philosophical traditions. The temptation and anxiety to overcome them, however, are not the case here. These schools of thought see in them potential paths for human development if only the anxiety is properly addressed and we learn what it reveals about us.

The concept of post-traumatic growth involves individuals becoming stronger after experiencing challenging situations. As a result, they gain, among other things, better relationships, more profound spirituality, and a stronger appreciation for life. Though anxiety is generally less intense than trauma, the same concepts might be relevant: going through challenges can turn into an opportunity to unveil the undiscovered potentials and viewpoints.

Carl Jung's analogy of "the wounded healer" suggests that our suffering becomes the main reason for our wisdom and, at the same time, compassion, making it possible for us to support others who have experienced similar challenges. In this context, the story of people who have battled anxiety and finally recovered is that they seek ways of helping people going through the same process, and in doing so, they find meaning in service and connection through support networks.

Japanese "mono no aware"—a term often referred to as the "Pathos of things" or the awareness of the impermanence of things—implies that even those lost in the transient nature of life can still find beauty and meaning. Such an outlook enables us to uncover feelings and material from our most difficult experiences, like anxiety, by viewing them as part of the broader spectrum of human life.

In much the same way, most mystics who discuss "nights of the soul" describe it as one of the rare paths leading to deeper spiritual understanding. These confused states of anxiety and spiritual emptiness are not referred to as failure signs but, instead, as calls for letting go of the shallow certainties and finding the intense sources of meaning and connection.

On the other hand, the existentialist point of view is that accepting responsibility means, among other things, being accountable for how we react to situations beyond our control. The truth is, even if we do not get the anxiety, we have the power to pick the kind of road that will link us with it and to find new meanings in it.

A few people would even say that their anxiety is a form of sensitiveness, which, despite being at times uncomfortable, makes their empathy, creativity, and consciousness of even the most minor things that others could overlook grow. Anxiety reframed as a way to turn from being exclusively negatively treated by the person who suffers from it into a potentially helpful sensitivity can considerably change one's relationship with it.

The spiritual emphasis on the gratitude practice is that it can, at the very least, uncover the silver lining that people might otherwise miss, even in the midst of troubles. Instead of being grateful for anxiety per se, however, the person may feel thankful for the insights, connections, and growth that the individual may experience as a result of learning to master anxiety.

Prayer and Contemplative Practices

Prayer is one of the main instruments that serve in dealing with anxiety symptoms through the loop of different spiritual traditions. This is because it provides both emotional regulation and a sense of connection to sources of support and meaning beyond the individual self.

Though prayer practices are distinct from one tradition to another, most of them share common themes. These common elements found in various religious prayers focus on sigh management.

Through intercessory prayer, individuals ask for help from God, receiving emotional relief by voicing their concerns and requesting assistance. Articulating worries as prayers and hopes can bring relief and clarity.

A prayer of thanks redirects the anxious person's attention from focusing on life's dangers and what is lacking to the awareness of the good that is already present. This practice serves as a perfect interrupter for the cycle of anxious ruminations by redirecting attention to the positive aspects of the experience. Some traditions have formalized gratitude practices, which can be utilized during crisis periods.

One example of contemplative prayer is the Centering Prayer in the Jesuit tradition, or the Jesus Prayer in the Orthodox Church, both of which are repetitive word or phrase practices designed to bring tranquility and stillness to the practitioner's mind. These measures not only provide a haven for anxious thoughts but also develop a capacity for serenity.

Prayer meditation through sacred texts or divine qualities offers solace to worried minds, bringing them closer to faiths that have been the mainstay of people struggling even in the most challenging times in history. The method of Christianity's lectio divina, as well as Islamic respect for the 99 names of Allah, provides a framework for one's meditation-driven prayer, not only in thought but also in word.

Social prayers and worship are the direct way that loneliness, which is the cause of anxiety, can be cured, and thus isolation, which mainly worsens anxiety, can be eliminated.

One can get attached to others and the joint meditation, Group prayer, or ceremony, more significant than any individual's concerns, is the way that an otherwise isolated person can now get connected with people and faiths larger than himself, which is a very important factor in alleviating anxiousness that is caused by loneliness.

Various faiths are endowed with practices such as the Sacrament of Confession or examination of conscience, which can significantly contribute to anxiety and may cause feelings of guilt, regret, or other moral concerns.

Quiet thinking, or "being with God," is an activities that help individuals live comfortably with uncertainty and unknowable consequences. These methods, through the very idea of not knowing, slowly build anxiety that requires sudden replies and unmistakable results.

Prayer walks or other meditative movement exercises offer all the benefits of prayer, plus they incorporate physical activity and a connection with nature. If a person is so anxious that they cannot sit still, then these are the best for them.

Designing One's Own Spiritual Practices

Anxiety can be better managed if one develops a personal spiritual practice, which does not necessarily have to be part of a formal religious tradition.

It has been observed that specific individuals are remarkably successful in developing innovative spiritual practices that reflect their own unique understanding of truth and values.

Experimentation is typically the first step in developing a personal practice. Individuals can try meditation, prayer, contemplative reading, or nature-based spiritual practices to explore their spiritual journey. By adopting this experimental method, we acknowledge the individual differences and do not assume that any single practice is suitable for everyone.

More often than not, consistency is more important than the duration of a spiritual practice. Daily brief practices are usually more beneficial than longer but irregular ones. In fact, starting with just five or ten minutes of daily spiritual practice can lay a foundation that can be developed over time.

Practices that are seasonal and cyclical respect the natural patterns of life, and they can provide a valuable framework for spiritual growth. Some people may find solace in practices that acknowledge solstices and equinoxes, moon phases, or other natural cycles as moments of introspection and spiritual focus.

The spiritual functions present in creative expressions, such as art, music, or poetry, offer modes that are entirely different from verbal or analytical ones in dealing with anxiety, yet they are hardly recognizable. These practices can reveal the same spiritual insights and bring about the healing that the cognitive-only approach would have otherwise missed.

Spiritual service to others is often undertaken; as a result, people gain a different view of the world, their anxieties, and are usually provided with a new sense of life. Helping others is what most people turn to in times of trouble; it provides relief from their own anxieties and worries, allowing them to shift their focus from themselves to others and experience a sense of purpose.

Practices related to nature are becoming increasingly successful in discovering spiritual elements through connection with the natural world. Nature watching, where people are aware of natural cycles and recognize their place within ecological systems, can provide perspective and peace, thereby reducing anxiety.

Firstly, spiritual and religious texts of the past and present can be an inexhaustible source of light, wisdom, and practical advice in the fight against anxiety. In addition, spirituality through intellectual means can be an excellent choice for those persons who not only want to experience but also understand the concepts.

Collage With Professional Support

Faith and philosophical ways of dealing with anxiety may work alongside but should never replace professional mental health treatment, which is most proper. The combined use of spiritual exercises with therapy, medication if necessary, and other treatments based on evidence is often considered to be the most comprehensive way of dealing with anxiety.

Additionally, many therapists who are aware of a client's spiritual beliefs and practices are sensitive to them as potential resources for healing, rather than obstacles to treatment, and are trained to work closely with clients to address these beliefs and practices. Therapy can be beneficial if an individual seeks a therapist who can understand and accept their spiritual direction.

Moreover, spiritual activities can support the anxiety treatment done by other professionals. Besides providing more coping resources, spirituality addresses the existential dimensions of anxiety that symptom-focused approaches might not be able to catch. For instance, meditative activities can heighten the capability to apply cognitive-behavioral techniques. In contrast, spiritual meaning-making can serve as a source of energy for exposure therapy or other complex treatments.

Religious or spiritually inclined counselors, chaplains, and spiritual directors can offer superior assistance to individuals whose anxiety stems from a spiritual nature or who wish to address the issue through spiritual means. These experts, while helping one through their spiritual exercise, can be alert to the fact that additional mental health support may be beneficial. Support groups that focus on spirituality, such as 12-step-based ones or those formed within religious communities, can offer not only the support of their members but also spiritual resources that may help manage anxiety. First of all, these groups can provide practical anxiety management strategies as well as spiritual support from other group members who have similar beliefs and experiences.

Integration requires the insight to recognize the most effective approach in the most suitable circumstances. Individuals sometimes find that initial anxiety increases due to their spiritual practices as they cause the appearance of difficult questions or feelings. The presence of a professional spiritual guide or therapist can make these situations more straightforward to handle productively.

Integration's aim is not to remove anxiety wholly, but rather to create a comprehensive toolset that would help a person to deal with anxiety when it happens. Serenity and philosophy can provide the context, meaning, and practice that help turn anxiety into a manageable hurdle to overcome along the spiritual path.

Practical Applications and Daily Practices

The revelations of religion and philosophy become particularly strong when they are transformed into practical approaches that can be applied in everyday life. This section describes and explains the various practices people may use when experimenting with different situations and beliefs.

Spiritual morning practices can lay the foundation for a tranquil and meaningful life that lasts the whole day. These are simple meditation, prayer, gratitude practice, or reading motivating texts. A mere five minutes of spiritual exercise at the start of the day can transform the entire day from one of anxiety to one of centeredness.

Night practices can provide people with time to reflect and prepare for a night's rest. These may include reflecting on the day with a heart full of gratitude, offering prayers or intentions for the next day. Evening spiritual practices can facilitate the processing of the day's journey and lower anxiety that can lead to sleep problems.

Workplace spirituality practices can provide time for calmness and insight to emerge during times of intense pressure. They might include short breathing exercises, silent prayers, or mantras, as well as contemplating transitions between activities or moments of gratitude. These practices should be rearranged to fit the workplace's constraints, but can still offer considerable relief.

Sacred pauses during the day thus allow one to draw on spiritual resources when the workload becomes overwhelming. These breaks turn down the volume on our anxiety and reconnect us to our bigger goals.

Facing anxiety with spirituality can reshape the manner in which we handle the pressure. Brief spiritual exercises can be a source of grounding and perspective. Prayer for wisdom, deep breathing for meditation, or recalling teachings that emphasize compassion and impermanence are examples of such practices.

Community spiritual practices help overcome the feeling of loneliness that is always there in the case of anxiety. They may involve attendance at religious services, meditation groups, study groups, or service projects. Community practices not only provide support but also connect individuals with traditions and wisdom that transcend the person, making personal concerns secondary.

One can resort to spiritual reading or study to get inspiration and to get out of anxiety. The person might engage in the spirituality of tradition, read contemporary spiritual writers, or explore the common ground between spirituality and psychology. As a result of the regular study of spiritual reading, one's understanding deepens, and in hard times, there are also resources.

Creating sacred spaces at home can be one of the most effective ways to maintain regular spiritual practices. It can be as simple as using a section of the room for meditation or prayer, or perhaps decorating the altar or shrine with the most beautiful and sacred items. Besides all this, it may just be a place that you identify as peaceful and conducive to spiritual reflection. Having a sacred space of your own will make your spiritual practice easily accessible and regular.

Ritual and ceremony can forever change personalities by remembering the past and linking the present with the future, especially after such occurrences that bring anxiety. These could be traditional ones that have been neglected for a long time and then revived only at specific times of the year or personal milestone events, transforming into rituals or simple daily ceremonies, such as lighting a candle or expressing gratitude.

People can process their emotions through ritual, which simultaneously connects them with meanings that extend beyond the self.

Conclusion: The Transformative Power of Meaning

Among all the spiritual and philosophical ways of suffering, anxiety is the most widely discussed. Management strategies are ways of turning the experience of anxiety into a source of growth, wisdom, and connection. So instead of finding relief, they ask us to find out what our anxiety might be teaching us and how it can serve us.

The first of the many common points shared by the different traditions presented in this chapter is that they all fundamentally acknowledge suffering and uncertainty as unavoidable parts of human life. They also recognize that striving to eliminate them is futile and antagonizing in nature. Secondly, they imply that the way we relate to tough times is what really matters, not the tough times themselves. Thirdly, they offer certain practices along with specific viewpoints that can lead to a change in one's relationship with anxiety, shifting from struggling against it to acceptance, from feeling lonely to making contact with others, and from feeling empty to finding purpose.

Many of these traditions also encompass the notion that anxiety is often a leading indicator of the existential depth of life's concerns, death, and humanity's place in the universe. Treating just the symptom of the disease by using medicine may provide only a temporary relief and miss the opportunities for a person to grow and learn, because anxiety may be pointing to new things to discover.

The experimental applications discussed in this chapter demonstrate that insights from thought and faith can be applied to everyday activities, which not only alleviate anxiety but also contribute to overall life meaning and satisfaction. The usage of these rituals does not work due to the elimination of anxiety, but via the provision of context, tools, and views that render anxiety more manageable and possibly significant.

Once more, it needs to be emphasized that, among other things, spiritual and philosophical means are not alternatives to professional mental health care. Some therapy, medication, or other professional help may accompany the case of severe anxiety.

Nevertheless, spiritual and philosophical approaches can complement other treatments and enhance various aspects of human experience that purely clinical approaches cannot.

Profoundly personal and experimental nature of the process, which involves anxiety and spiritual as well as philosophical means, to find out what strategies are accurate and helpful. It is not relevant how much one follows the teachings of a particular religious school. Still, it is the readiness to discover how anxiety can lead to a deeper understanding, helping, and feeling closer to others that is important.

Perhaps most importantly, these methods see anxiety as a signal that the person has not failed or is not weak, but rather, this feeling is a natural reaction to the fact that life is full of problems and is uncertain. This different perspective on the issue may provide the person with significant relief while also opening up new possibilities for growth and a deeper understanding than they had before.

The search for meaning in the spiritual and philosophical realms ultimately results in a fundamental truth: we are not separate individuals who fight our battles alone but are, instead, the characters of a bigger story of human bonding through, which has been the primary source of life for human beings throughout history, and by which humans have been able to find meaning and get through hardships.

The acknowledgment of this truth might make us realize that our anxiety may be the cause of our being more connected with life and people rather than the reason why we are apart from them. Our conclusion here is the ending of the journey, which means the invitation to keep trying out and experimenting with the various ways and views that resonate with one's life experience and conviction, and being prepared for the fact that anxiety might be the cause of our learning, guidance, and enlightenment, albeit being uncomfortable.

This alteration might be the greatest gift of spiritual and philosophical views: the potential to see the world as a source of meaning and beauty, which is the very essence of the human experience, despite its extreme and demanding aspects.

Glossary of Key Terms

A

Acceptance and Commitment Therapy (ACT): A method of therapy that deals with the acceptance of complicated feelings instead of trying to get rid of them, and at the same time being involved in the activities that are according to one's personal values.

All-or-Nothing Thinking: A cognitive distortion that depicts characters of a situation/issue in either-or aspects, be it good or bad, without any middle ground (for example, considering that a person is either perfect or a complete failure).

Amygdala: A tiny, almond-shaped brain area that functions as the brain's early warning system; thus, it initiates an anxiety response when it detects a potential threat.

Anticipatory Anxiety: A Feeling of nervousness regarding the possibility of getting anxiety or panic attacks in the future, which can turn into a loop where the fear of anxiety causes more anxiety.

Avoidance Cycle: A repetitive action where the avoidance of anxiety-provoking situations gives a feeling of temporary relief, but on the other hand, it also strengthens anxiety over time and, therefore, it stops the person from learning that the situation may not be dangerous.

B

Beta-blockers: The medications that can hide the physical symptoms of anxiety (such as rapid heartbeat and trembling) and which are sometimes given to patients with performance anxiety.

Benzodiazepines: Short-acting anti-anxiety drugs that work almost instantly, giving only acute anxiety symptom relief, but are mainly advised to be used for a limited period because of the potential for dependence.

Box Breathing: This is a breathing exercise that involves four distinct phases: inhalation, holding, exhalation, and holding the lungs empty (typically 4-4-4-4), all with precise timing, to produce a sense of calm and concentration.

C

Catastrophic Thinking: One of the cognitive distortions that reckons worst-case scenarios as the only outcome and that you won't be able to cope with it.

Cognitive Behavioral Therapy (CBT): A method of therapy that is extensively recognized and mainly centers on the identification of thought patterns and behaviors that lead to anxiety, as well as changing them.

Cognitive Distortions: The leading cause of anxiety is these exaggerated or inaccurate thought patterns, which include catastrophic thinking, all-or-nothing thinking, mind-reading, and fortune-telling.

Compulsions: The incessant doing of certain things or mental recitations, which are done as a means of relieving the anxiety that is caused by the appearance of disturbing thoughts in Obsessive-Compulsive Disorder.

D

Dialectical Behavior Therapy (DBT): A therapy that emphasizes the development of skills in mindfulness, distress tolerance, emotional regulation, and interpersonal effectiveness, thereby enabling patients to manage their emotions more effectively.

Diaphragmatic Breathing: Also known as belly breathing, this method involves breathing through the diaphragm, allowing for a deeper and more effective inhalation. This is typically done to enable the body to be most relaxed, with the chest not engaged and the body's relaxation response activated.

Distress Tolerance: The capability of enduring the most challenging moments that life can bring without making the situation worse by engaging in impulsive or destructive ways of dealing with it.

Dive Response: A vagus nerve stimulation method, which consists of one technique where the face is immersed in cold water to help trigger the parasympathetic nervous system, which is a calming one, hence the relaxation of anxiety, and that is why the dive response is so effective.

E

Emotional Regulation: The capacity to successfully deal with feelings that one is not able to completely push away nor be fully controlled by them at the same time.

Exposure and Response Prevention (ERP): A method of treatment for OCD where the patient first exposes himself to obsessive thoughts and, at the same time, refrains from the performance of compulsive behaviors.

Exposure Therapy: An approach to treatment that includes a gradual, systematic, and detailed confrontation of the most dreaded situations or objects in a controlled, supportive environment.

Eye Movement Desensitization and Reprocessing (EMDR): The specific and efficient method of treatment for trauma-related anxiety, which involves the processing of traumatic memories along with the engagement in bilateral stimulation.

F

Fight-or-Flight Response: The physiological response of the body, which is automatic and thus happens as soon as the senses detect a threat. It comprises not only increased heart rate, but also faster breathing, muscle contraction, and so on, all of which aim to help one survive the danger.

Fortune Telling: A cognitive distortion where a person is seen to be predicting adverse outcomes as the only result to happen with absolute certainty, even if the future is unknown.

4-7-8 Breathing: A breathing method that involves one inhaling a breath for four counts, holding for 7, and exhaling for 8, forming a complete breath. This way of breathing is pronounced as the best by most people in cases of acute anxiety.

G

Generalized Anxiety Disorder (GAD): A disorder marked by the habit of worrying, the person, far from quitting, will worry about multiple, even unrelated, topics one after another.

Grounding Techniques: Methods that introduce focus to the present moment and, as a consequence, stop the continuous spiral of anxiety by sensory or cognitive engagement with an immediate physical reality.

H

Health Anxiety: A fixation on the possibility of having or getting serious diseases that can be life-threatening, and very frequently, the person with this disorder tends to interpret very normal body changes as a sign of a dangerous disease.

Hypervigilance: Such a condition of over-excitement of alertness and thorough scrutiny of the surroundings for any danger is typical of anxiety disorders and trauma responses.

M

Mental Filtering: This term refers to a cognitive distortion in which a person selectively remembers only the negative aspects of a situation, often overlooking the positive or neutral facts.

Mind Reading: A cognitive distortion referring to the assumption of knowing the thoughts of others. Generally, it is believed that the thoughts are about the person in a negative way.

Mindfulness: The process of experiencing the thoughts, feelings, and sensations with full and current-living awareness and not judging.

O

Obsessions: Unrelenting, intrusive thoughts that eventually cause anxiety in

Obsessive-Compulsive Disorder (OCD): A disorder that comes with intrusive, unwanted thoughts (obsessions), and repetitive behaviors or mental acts (compulsions)

that are done to decrease the anxiety level.

Opposite Action: An approach that consists of doing the contrary of what an emotion is prompting you to do, in cases when the emotion is not playing out effectively or is causing harm.

P

Panic Attack: A terrifying moment when a person's anxiety grows very high (at the time, rapid heart rate, sweating, shivering, shortness of breath, and fear of losing control or death).

Panic Disorder: A situation in which rare panic attacks evolve into a condition of constant dread over the possibility of more attacks (anticipatory anxiety).

Parasympathetic Nervous System: The body part in charge of "rest and digest" functions that bring on calm and neutralize the fight-or-flight effect.

Personalization: One of the distortions of cognition that causes an individual to assume responsibility for events that are outside one's control and not primarily about them.

Post-Traumatic Growth: Bright side psychological changes that may happen due to encountering challenging situations.

Post-Traumatic Stress Disorder (PTSD): A disorder that may appear after the sufferer has gone through the traumatic event or has seen it happen, with the symptoms being involuntary memories, avoidance, changes in mood, and overreaction.

Progressive Muscle Relaxation (PMR): The method of working through different muscle groups, tensing and then letting them go to release the tension that has built up, and thus achieve physical relaxation.

R

Radical Acceptance: Recognizing the truth of things as they are instead of how you want them to be, without acceptance, but still without any extra suffering from not conflicting with the circumstances.

Resilience: One's ability to go through life with difficult emotions, experiences, and failures without losing overall well-being and not stopping at moving forward in a meaningful way.

S

Safety Behaviors: The acts that you do to feel safe in a situation where you are likely to be anxious, which, in fact, stop you from discovering that the problem is not dangerous.

Separation Anxiety: Extremely scared of being apart from attachment figures or places that are familiar to them. Both children and adults recognize the condition.

Should Statements: A thought process that leads to anxiety and pressure by requiring that things should be other than they are.

Social Anxiety: Anxiety from social activities, especially when you are to be judged, embarrassed, or rejected by others.

Specific Phobias: The fear is so intense that the victim's behavior will feature complete avoidance of the feared object or situation.

SSRIs/SNRIs: Medications used to treat depressive symptoms (Selective Serotonin Reuptake Inhibitors and Serotonin-Norepinephrine Reuptake Inhibitors) that are prescribed as a first-line treatment for anxiety disorders.

T

TIPP Technique: A distress tolerance skill that consists of changing one's Temperature, doing very Intense exercise, paced breathing, and paired muscle relaxation to manage the feeling of panic.

V

Vagus Nerve: The cranial nerve that is the furthest and is the leading cause of the parasympathetic nervous system. Hence, it can be easily stimulated by a few practices like cold exposure, humming, and gentle neck stretches to bring down anxiety.

W

Worry Time: A controlled way by which one could allocate a specific time for dealing with things that bother him, instead of the worry getting the whole day to invade his thoughts.

www.ingramcontent.com/pod-product-compliance
Lightning Source LLC
Chambersburg PA
CBHW060928040426
42445CB00011B/842